Faithful unto Death

T0015675

Faithful unto Death

Polycarp

David Luckman

CF4·K

10 9 8 7 6 5 4 3 2 1

Copyright © 2023 David Luckman
Paperback ISBN: 978-1-5271-1029-8
Ebook ISBN: 978-1-5271-1062-5

Published by Christian Focus Publications,
Geanies House, Fearn, Tain, Ross-shire,
IV20 1TW, Scotland, U.K.
www.christianfocus.com;
email: info@christianfocus.com

Cover design by Daniel van Straaten
Cover illustration by Graham Kennedy
Printed and bound by Nørhaven, Denmark

Contents

The Hideout

Fight or flight is the natural response to the threat of danger. Polycarp was not inclined to adopt either position, even though his enemies were looking to kill him. As the Bishop of Smyrna, Polycarp intended to stay in his beloved city. His strong faith in Jesus Christ would help him face his enemies with steadfastness and courage. The elders of the Smyrnaean church, however, preferred he hid from his foes.

'Bishop, you must flee Smyrna. The mob is crying out for the blood of Christians in the city, and it would be a great travesty if you should die at the hands of these devils,' said Marcus, one of the church elders.

'I will not run away,' replied Polycarp. 'My people need me during this dark hour.'

'You will be no good to them dead,' said another elder.

'Our Lord warned us in the Scriptures of these days of tribulation. I am not afraid to die,' said Polycarp.

'No one doubts your faithfulness, bishop, even to death,' said Marcus reassuringly, 'but there is no need to placate the bloodthirstiness of the mob. Please consider leaving the city. I know of an abandoned farm not that far outside the city. It is quite hidden, and you will be safe there for a while,' said Marcus.

'At least until the Festival of Hellenes is over,' added the other elder.

'And no one will think that you are running away. You are our bishop, and we love you and need you to help us keep walking the straight path of the Lord, as you have always done,' said Marcus.

The plea from the elders of the Smyrnaean church came at the time when Smyrna was crowded with pilgrims. There were business people among them; traders, and bankers, all wise in the ways of the world and familiar with the power of Rome. They were keen to serve and exploit the visitors to the city, who had come from all over Asia Minor for the Festival of Hellenes. This festival was organised by the League of Hellenes which was an association of representatives from the leading cities of the province. The four chief cities were Ephesus, Pergamum, Smyrna, and Miletus. The annual Festival of Hellenes was held in each of these cities in turn.

Each and every day of the festival, the stadium was packed with over twenty thousand shouting spectators, all eager to be entertained. Like all the stadia throughout the empire, the Smyrnaean stadium was a splendid building, decorated with gold, silver, and precious stones. There were statues of early

Roman emperors lining the walkway – men like Augustus, meaning 'exalted one'; Caligula, the violent and unpredictable ruler; Hadrian, who built a wall across the width of England; and the present Emperor Antonius Pius. These stadia were designed by emperors and ambitious nobility to offer Games to the citizens of the Roman provinces. Arenas could seat thousands of spectators for special events such as chariot races and athletic meetings. It also gave the people an opportunity to frantically gamble their money on potential winners. It kept them happy. A contented population didn't cause many problems for the Roman authorities.

The bloodlust of the crowds grew over the years, as they sought more vicious forms of amusement. New Games were offered. They were battles between gladiators. There was nothing like the spilling of human blood to quench the mob's thirst for violent entertainment. Gladiators often fought to the death in front of cheering crowds who loved every brutal moment of their scrap. These gladiators were usually slaves, criminals, or prisoners of war. Sometimes special volunteers would seek the title of gladiator. All of them were trained in elite camps that would prepare them for combat in the arena. They would learn how to use a sword, trident, or other weapon that could be used to kill the opponent. If a gladiator was wounded in a battle, the crowds would exercise the power of life or death over the injured. They would wave hankies to spare the life of the incapacitated warrior. But if they were so inclined, a thumbs down would signal their displeasure, giving permission for his opponent to dispatch him to the afterlife.

Each morning in the stadium, the day's activities began with a loyal demonstration of devotion to the Emperor, Antonius Pius. Incense would be burned as a fragrant offering with the words, 'Caesar is Lord'. It provided an excellent opportunity for an outcry against Christians who were hated in the Roman province of Asia Minor and good targets for persecution.

The gospel of Jesus Christ had been faithfully preached in Asia Minor since the apostle Paul proclaimed it in Ephesus over a hundred years ago. The churches had grown by the grace of God. By now it was common knowledge that Christians would never say, 'Caesar is Lord.' For them, Jesus is the only Lord of life. So it was easy to accuse people of being Christians and of rebellion against Caesar's rule. Often the authorities had some amusement putting the believers' loyalty to Christ to the test. If they recanted and convinced the Roman leadership that they were no longer Christians, they would be pardoned. But if their faith in Christ was proved genuine, then they would be punished. Perhaps sentenced to prison or even death! Surely if the Christians were going to die, why not make a spectacle of them, and throw them to the beasts in the arena? It would make for good sport, at the very least.

During the Games in Smyrna, crowds started to demand the death of Christians. The roar would go up,

'Away with the Christians! Away with the Christians!' each cry getting louder than before. The din was deafening.

It was on a cold and crisp February morning in A.D. 156[1] that thousands of people walked excitedly into the stadium in Smyrna for the beginning of the Games, which were an important part of the Festival of Hellenes. Some made accusations against a number of Christians who had travelled for the festival celebrations from Philadelphia, about eighty-five miles east of Smyrna. It was a terrifying ordeal for those who loved Christ. At the same time, the excitement was palpable.

The Christians believed that to die for Christ was a truly honourable death. Some even sought the martyr's path, like a Phrygian Christian called Quintus, who was caught up in the exhilaration of it all. He even managed to persuade some others to be arrested for the sake of Christ. The soldiers arrested them, and they were put into the local prison until they could be examined by the authorities.

The elders pleaded with Polycarp that he should immediately leave his home and go somewhere safe, preferably out of the city. However, they had little time to argue, as the Roman death squad was being rounded up to hunt for the bishop. In the end, Polycarp relented. He relocated to a derelict farmhouse in the countryside, not too far from the city. He had a handful

---

1. *Anno Domini* – 'in the year of our Lord'

of trusted attendants to care for him – three men and two younger boys.

The abandoned farmhouse had been empty for many years, that is, until now. The fugitive Polycarp was angry, frustrated and deeply saddened by the turn of events in his beloved hometown of Smyrna.

'How long do I have to hide in this awful place?' he asked.

'Until this whole thing dies down,' replied Lucas, his trusted assistant.

'This whole thing, as you call it, is the persecution and killing of the Lord's people,' Polycarp said in mild rebuke. 'I am the leader of the church here in Smyrna. As I said before, it is not right that I should flee my home, when our brothers and sisters in Christ are imprisoned and murdered for their faith in our Lord. You know how bloodthirsty the mob gets, especially during the Games of the Festival of Hellenes. Some may even die.'

'Bishop Polycarp,' began Lucas his attendant, 'it is really important for us that you should live. You teach us the Scriptures and exhort us to walk in the ways of the Lord. We need you and we would all be heartbroken if you should die, especially at the hands of the Romans.'

'You should know well enough by now, Lucas, that those who live in Christ Jesus, never see each other for the last time when death comes.' Lucas nodded in agreement. He loved the wisdom of the old bishop.

The small farmhouse that provided sanctuary for Polycarp and his attendants had fallen foul of bad weather, too much rainfall and numerous pest infestations which contributed to the failure of the arable crops there. Still, the derelict farm made for a good hideout.

The main room, or atrium, was dirty and dank due to its abandonment. In its heyday, this room was the hub of family life. The family would have taken their meals, entertained friends, cooked the food and worshipped household gods in this room. The atrium was open to the sky in the centre, where a square hole in the roof admitted light and air and allowed the smoke of the fire to escape. The roof sloped inwards and there was a shallow pool in the floor to catch rainwater. A small kitchen had been added, suggesting that the farm had some success in the past to allow the farmer to increase the size of the dwelling. Adding smaller rooms was a common practice for those whose position in society improved.

When the men arrived at the farmhouse, they found some wooden chairs strewn over the floor. On first inspection the chairs looked sturdy enough to hold a man's weight. There was a draughty bedroom upstairs due to a hole in the corner wall of the room. It could be easily plugged with some broken bricks and timber that were lying around the place. Then at least the bishop would have a room to sleep in which would give him a bit of privacy and peace over the next few days.

The group began the work of tidying up the place to make it a bit more habitable for their short stay. Polycarp did not plan on being absent from his flock for more than a few days. He strongly felt the need to stay close to the church in Smyrna. Before he left, he promised them that he would not be too far away and that he would earnestly pray for them. He would beg God to be their refuge and strength in their hour of need.

Lucas finished fixing a small fire and positioned some of the chairs around it. 'It is important to rest now, bishop,' said Lucas. 'It has been a difficult day and I know that you are tired. I shall make you something to eat before you retire to bed.' Lucas disappeared to prepare supper. Max was already in the kitchen trying to tidy up a bit, with the support of two younger boys who wanted to help the bishop in any way they could at this time. Young Max had not been in Polycarp's service for long. He nodded at Lucas as he entered the room. The other two boys just ignored him and got on with clearing any debris from the kitchen surfaces.

After a short while, Lucas appeared with the supper he had promised to make Polycarp before bed. 'There you go, bishop,' he said as he gently placed a small plate of food on a table next to the old man's chair.

'Thank you, Lucas,' said Polycarp. 'Please sit with me for a moment,' he said pointing to a chair opposite. Lucas sat down.

'I cannot get Quintus out of my head,' said Polycarp, as Lucas tried to make himself as comfortable as possible on the cold wooden chair.

'Yes, Quintus,' sighed Lucas.

'I do not approve of his actions,' said Polycarp, 'nor those of his companions.'

'Neither do the church elders,' added Lucas.

'No one has the right to snatch at martyrdom,' said Polycarp. Lucas could hear some mild exasperation in the bishop's voice. Polycarp leaned forward. 'It is for the Lord, and for the Lord only, to choose who should suffer for his name,' he said. 'Do these people think that they will receive honour in the eyes of the Church for doing such a witless thing?' It was a rhetorical question. 'Who volunteers to the Romans to be made a spectacle of?!' he exclaimed. That was also a rhetorical question.[2]

Once again, Lucas nodded in agreement. There was a moment of silence. Lucas noticed that the bishop had not yet reached for his food. 'Eat something to keep your strength up,' he said.

'Yes, yes, I will,' said Polycarp agreeably. He took a piece of bread from his plate and popped it in his mouth.

At that moment another attendant appeared in the room. 'I have prepared your bed, Bishop Polycarp,' he said.

---

2. A *rhetorical question* is a question that someone asks for effect but doesn't expect anyone to answer it.

'Thank you very much, Adrian,' replied Polycarp. He did not know what he would do without his faithful and trusted attendants. They had served the ageing bishop for many years and loved him like a father. Polycarp had never married nor had children, and yet he looked upon these young men as his sons in Christ. Lucas and Adrian were not that young, but everyone seemed young to the eighty-six-year-old bishop! Adrian disappeared into the kitchen, where some others were taking the time to clean, not knowing how long the group would be staying there. Polycarp watched him walk across the room. Then he turned his gaze once more upon Lucas.

'I am getting tired,' he said. 'Tomorrow, we shall gather early for prayer. We must be especially urgent in prayer at this time, Lucas. There is much that we must bring before our heavenly Father on our knees.'

'Yes, bishop, of course. I shall make sure that we will be ready to pray when you arise.'

Polycarp got up and walked to the stairs. Then he stopped. 'Remember, Lucas if we are to affect any change in this world, we must begin with prayer. And our persecuted brothers and sisters in Christ need our prayers.'

The old bishop climbed the creaky stairs slowly, the light from the candle in his hand guiding his steps. He knelt by the side of his bed, said his prayers then read the Scriptures. He snuffed out the candle and got into bed. It took quite a while before he drifted off to sleep, but his sleep was disturbed. It was a strange bed in a strange house. His mind was racing with the torrid events of the Games – the arrests of Christians and their impending executions. Polycarp was deeply concerned for the wellbeing of his flock. As their shepherd, under the loving rule of Jesus Christ, the Good Shepherd, it was his duty to protect them.

The next morning, Polycarp woke as the sunlight streamed through the window into his bedchamber. He arose, dressed, and went downstairs. The small group of helpers were waiting for him to pray, as Lucas promised.

Polycarp greeted them with a smile. 'Good morning,' he said. 'There is much to pray for. Our brothers and sisters are being persecuted at the Games. We must pray for them, that they will stand strong in the faith of Christ Jesus, and not buckle under the weight of intimidation they will receive from the proconsul,[3] Statius Quadratus.'

Polycarp looked at the faces of the few fellow believers before him. They were sombre and deeply troubled by the vicious events that were unfolding at the stadium in Smyrna.

'We must pray for the proconsul too,' added Polycarp.

'Why must we?' asked Max dispassionately.

'It is a simple command from our Lord Jesus, my young Max. "Love your enemies. And pray for those

---

3. A *proconsul* is the title given to someone who governs a region of the Roman Empire.

17

who persecute you, that you may be sons of your Father who is in heaven," says the Lord Jesus.'[4]

'It's not that easy, bishop, when we see how they kill us!' blurted out Lucas in exasperation.

'I know,' said Polycarp softly.

'You heard the reports of Germanicus before the proconsul,' Lucas said. 'Unlike that snivelling Quintus who recanted his love of Christ the moment he saw the wild beasts in the stadium. His cowardice and betrayal did a lot to dishearten the believers, Bishop. They told us as much.'

'And yet Germanicus would not offer incense to Caesar,' added Adrian. 'He stood before the proconsul and boldly proclaimed his love for the Master, and they threw him to the beasts. He was eaten alive. It was sheer wickedness, bishop.'

'All the while, the mob is howling, "away with the Christians!" said Lucas. 'Then they shout, "Where is Polycarp? Hunt out Polycarp!" I mean, that's why we are here in this … this …' Lucas was trying to find the words to describe their hideout, when Polycarp motioned with his hand to calm his young attendant then looked solemnly at the others.

'How difficult is the love of God,' he gently said, placing his hand on Lucas's shoulder, 'but we seek to obey the Lord in all things. As Christians, we trust in the Lord, and we obey his commands, even when it is hard for us to do at times. But we must do it. We are

---

4. Matthew 5:44-45.

the Lord's servants.' Polycarp paused for a moment and sat down in an empty chair. 'It is right for us to pray for the proconsul and his soldiers. We must pray that the Lord would soften their hard hearts and be open to hearing the good news of Jesus. Perhaps the Lord will allow one of his people to present the gospel to Statius and his men. We can pray that their blind eyes be opened to see Jesus and bow down and worship him.'

Polycarp really wanted his enemies to know the Lord personally. Imagine what Smyrna would be like if the authorities were believers. What a wonderful difference it would make to the city. The men knelt on the floor and began to pray for the church under attack in Smyrna, and not only in that city, but in the cities, towns, and villages around the Roman Empire.

A Letter to Smyrna

As evening approached, the temperature dropped to only a few degrees above zero. The small group of men had been praying all day. It was now time for something to eat. Adrian managed to get a fire going in the hearth. Lucas was prepping the evening meal. Max took the opportunity to find out something about Polycarp and his great friend the apostle John.

'What was the apostle like?' asked Max.

Polycarp smiled. 'The apostle John was a wonderful man,' he said.

'Did he ever talk about the day he found the tomb of Jesus empty?'

'He spoke about it often. The empty grave of our Lord Jesus is a very crucial part of our faith,' said Polycarp.

'Because we do not follow a dead Christ, isn't that right, bishop?'

'That is exactly right, Max,' agreed Polycarp. 'Christ is risen! Alleluia!' His voice was loud and strong.

'Alleluia!' came the reply from the kitchen. The other two men joined in the response! Then Lucas said half-jokingly, 'keep your voice down, bishop. We don't want to attract any unwanted visitors.'

'Yes, yes, of course,' replied Polycarp sheepishly. A quiet descended upon the farmhouse but it was momentary. Max wanted to know more about Polycarp's memories of the apostle John. He was fascinated about how the old bishop knew the apostle and also how John had influenced Polycarp's life.

'How old were you when you met John?' asked Max.

'I was just a young boy when I met John. My parents were Christians and had read his Gospel to me before we arrived from Syria. So I knew about him, and our Lord Jesus from his writing. They brought me with them to the church gatherings. I would often leave their side to sit with my friend, Papias. We would squirm our way through the people, trying to get as close as possible to where John would sit and teach the Scriptures.'

Adrian and Lucas came back into the room carrying plates of food and handed them out to the two men in front of the fire. Polycarp thanked God for the meal, and they began to eat. Max then looked at Polycarp. 'Is there anything in particular that you remember about those times in church?' he asked.

'I remember it all,' said Polycarp dramatically. The men smiled at one another. Max, Lucas and Adrian waited in anticipation for Polycarp to go on.

'I remember clearly John telling the church about one of the miracles that happened in Jerusalem. John and Peter were there to worship at the temple. It was the middle of the afternoon, and the people were coming together for prayer. A cripple was at one of the temple gates begging people for money as they entered. John told us that the man had been doing that for most of his life.'

'It must be terrible, having to beg people for money,' interrupted Max. 'I could never do that.'

'You would, if you had no other way of getting money,' said Adrian. 'The man had to survive somehow.'

'The apostles were cross that anyone should have to resort to begging. In the Scriptures, God told his people to be generous, and to look after each other.[1] But clearly the people did not listen,' said Polycarp. 'The crippled beggar was a constant reminder of their rebellion and neglect of the poorer people in their society.' Polycarp did not mince words. He went on. 'Of course, he asked Peter and John for money as they approached, but they didn't have any to give him. I'll never forget John's face as he told us what happened next. It radiated with compassion and love.' Polycarp paused as his admiration for his beloved pastor welled up.

'Go on, bishop,' said Max who was hanging on every word from the elderly preacher. 'What happened?'

---

1. Deuteronomy 15:7-11.

'I can remember John's gaze falling upon Papias and I as we sat at his feet in church. He told us what they said to the man. 'We do not have any money,' they said. 'But we will give you what we have … in the name of Jesus Christ of Nazareth, get up and walk.'

'What?!' exclaimed Max.

'That's what Papias and I said!' admitted Polycarp. 'John just smiled at us. Then he told us that Peter grabbed the beggar and got him up. Immediately strength came into the beggar's legs, ankles, and feet. The man went into the temple with the two apostles. He was jumping and leaping and yelling with glee. John said the man was giving thanks to God for his salvation. The apostles were holding on tightly to him, otherwise John thought he would have jumped and leaped right out of the temple and down the street!'

The men laughed. They could picture the scene in their mind's eye.

'Naturally a crowd arrived to see why there was such a commotion,' continued Polycarp.

'It's not surprising that a miraculous healing like that would draw a crowd,' said Adrian.

'You are absolutely right, Adrian,' said Polycarp, 'and the apostles took the opportunity to tell the people what had happened to the man. The Lord gave them the strength to speak up about Jesus.'

'What did they say?' asked Max.

'Well, as you can imagine, the people gawping at the healed man were totally amazed by it. They thought Peter and John had special powers. The apostles, however, wanted to correct that idea straight away. They told the people that it had nothing to do with their power or piety. Rather, the beggar was healed by the risen and ascended Jesus Christ,' said Polycarp.

'How did they react to that news?' asked Max.

'John said that the crowd was quiet. They were listening keenly to Peter as he went on to explain the gospel of Jesus. He called them to repent of their sins. He told them to turn back to God who would remember their sins no more. He spoke of a wonderful future in God's restored creation for all who would trust in the Saviour. He told them that they could know times of refreshing in their lives today because Christ Jesus is risen from the grave.'

'It really is good news, bishop!' declared Max. 'Did they receive it as such?'

'Yes, indeed they did,' said Polycarp. 'John told us that thousands became Christians that day.'

'Thousands?!' repeated Max in astonishment.

'Yes. About five thousand men,' said Polycarp.

'That's amazing!' exclaimed Max. Polycarp was enjoying the conversation with his young helper very much. It was a welcome distraction to the dastardly goings-on in Smyrna. 'Then what happened?' asked Max.

'Well, John testified that as they were speaking, a group of angry religious leaders came and arrested them.'

'But they weren't doing anything wrong,' said Max in a tone of exasperation.

'They were enraged because Peter and John were preaching about the risen Lord Jesus,' answered Polycarp. 'You see, Max, the religious leaders wanted to silence them. They wanted to stop the apostles from spreading the name of Jesus everywhere. They wanted to extinguish the fire of the Spirit before things got "out of hand" in their opinion.'

'So were they thrown into prison?'

'Yes. Maybe the religious leaders of the day thought they could easily crush Christianity before it got off the ground by threatening and persecuting the apostles. But, as we all know, this was not the case. God's Church has grown spiritually and numerically since then.'

'How did John feel about being imprisoned?' asked Max.

'He said it just made him and Peter braver,' said Polycarp. 'You'll find this throughout the New Testament, Max. The authorities lock up Christians, but the Christians talk all the more about our Lord Jesus. And the Word of God spreads.'

'So, how were they braver?' asked Max.

'They were brought before the High Priest and his priestly family. The religious leaders and educators of all Jerusalem were there too.'

'That's quite an intimidating group of people,' interjected Max.

'And yet when the men were asked, "by what power or by what name did you heal the crippled beggar?" Peter and John replied, "if you are interested in how this miracle took place, it's very simple, it was Jesus," and then they preached the gospel to them!' Polycarp was beaming now as he told the story. 'Then Peter said, "you are the builders of the religion in Israel. But if you leave Jesus out of everything, your building is going to crumble. It will appear religious on the outside, but unless Jesus is part of it, God will not be part of it. If you reject the risen Jesus, you reject the only salvation that God offers you. The very name that you wish to destroy, is your only hope. And all your religious ceremonies and all your prayers, apart from Jesus, are useless."'

'I doubt I could be as brave as that, facing such a hostile crowd, bishop,' admitted Max.

'The Lord gives the strength, Max,' assured the bishop. Then he continued. 'So, John said that they were warned not to speak in the name of Jesus again. But he and Peter told the council that they would flatly disobey because their obedience to Christ was greater than their obedience to the council.'

Max's jaw dropped in astonishment. 'Were they beaten or flogged for that answer?' he asked.

'No, they were just threatened.'

'They weren't punished?'

'The people were praising God because of the miracle. And the council were afraid to punish John and Peter in case the crowd turned against them. So, they just threatened the apostles instead and sent them on their way!'

As Polycarp and his attendants gave thanks to God for his mercy, their joy was interrupted by the sudden arrival of an elder from the church at Smyrna. The men were so engrossed in Polycarp's childhood recollection that they didn't hear him approach. They were alarmed by his presence and yet relieved that it wasn't a soldier from the city on the hunt for Polycarp.

'You startled us, Marcus!' declared Polycarp.

'I am sorry, bishop,' replied Marcus. 'However, you should be more careful. Have you forgotten that the authorities are looking for you?'

'We were reminiscing about the Lord's apostle, John, and got distracted,' replied Polycarp.

'You cannot afford to be distracted, bishop, certainly not at the moment,' chided Marcus.

Polycarp agreed. He turned to his attendants and said, 'I think that's enough for now. You know, John said at the end of his Gospel, that our Lord Jesus did so many wonderful things that if they were all written down in books, there wouldn't be enough space in the world to hold them.[2] Perhaps we can reminisce some more later.'

---

2. John 21:25.

'Marcus, did you make sure that you were not followed?' asked Lucas.

'I was very careful,' said Marcus. 'I have brought you some supplies.' Marcus handed the basket to Adrian, who placed it on the floor next to his chair.

'What's the news from Smyrna?' interjected Max. 'Is the proconsul furious that we have eluded the grasp of Rome?' he smirked.

'Constantly he has to calm that brutal public baying for the bishop's blood,' Marcus answered. 'He has lots of people out looking for all of you.' Marcus turned to the bishop, knelt before him, and gently clasped his frail hands. 'Bishop Polycarp, please consider moving further away from the city,' he begged.

Polycarp shook his head. 'No. I must be close to my flock,' he said, softly, 'and like those dear brothers and sisters in Christ who suffer during these barbaric events, I too must be "faithful unto death".'

Marcus was annoyed at Polycarp's obstinacy. 'I know you are quoting the Lord's command, bishop,' said Marcus, 'but you need not die yet.' His affection for the elderly bishop was in danger of being misconstrued for irritation.

Max looked at Marcus quizzically, as if to say, what command do you mean?

'Be faithful unto death is the command that Jesus gave to the church at Smyrna through the apostle John, while he was in exile on the island of Patmos roughly sixty years ago,' explained Marcus.

'John told us that the island was a hilly little place,' said Polycarp. 'Instead of being executed like the other apostles for following Jesus, he had been banished by the Roman authorities to Patmos. It was there, one evening, that he received a prophecy from the Lord Jesus, and he wrote it all down. It became known as the "Revelation to John".'

'This book of the Bible is very special to us because within the opening few chapters, there's a small letter from Christ to the church at Smyrna. The Lord said what he thought of the church in Smyrna, and it wasn't as bad a report as some of the surrounding churches in Asia Minor. But Jesus said the road ahead was going to be difficult,' said Marcus.

Polycarp had committed the letter to memory, and so he began to recite it to the small gathering:

And to the angel of the church in Smyrna write:
'The words of the first and the last, who died and came to life. I know your tribulation and your poverty (but you are rich) and the slander of those who say they are Jews and are not, but are a synagogue of Satan. Do not fear what you are about to suffer. Behold, the devil is about to throw some of you into prison, that you may be tested, and for ten days you will have tribulation. Be faithful unto death and I will give you the crown of life. He who has an ear, let him hear what the Spirit says to the churches. The one who conquers will not be hurt by the second death.'[3]

---

3. Revelation 2:8-11.

A brief silence followed as the men soaked in the words of the letter. Marcus then decided to give some background. He had lived in Smyrna all his life and was very familiar with the history of his home town. 'A temple was built to the *Dea Roma*[4] about 195 years before our Lord Jesus Christ was born,' he began. 'Around that time, our city of Smyrna was known for being very patriotic to Rome. But there were a lot of cities at the beginning of the last century who were competing for the privilege of building a temple to Emperor Tiberius, who was the leader of Rome at that time. This was how the cult of the Roman Empire started. It was a matter of great pride for Smyrna to build the temple.'

'Christians, however, would not burn incense to the emperor of Rome,' continued Polycarp. 'They would not call him Lord, because only Jesus Christ is Lord. As far as Smyrnaean culture was concerned, Christians were inflexible and unpatriotic. And so Christ's followers were worthy of persecution.'

Persecution wears many masks, just like the devil behind it. Sometimes he is hard to spot, posing as an angel of light. Other times there is no mistaking his identity.

'The hatred that the believers experienced because they refused to take part in emperor worship was fanned into flame by the local Jewish population. The Jews were exempt from emperor worship,' said Polycarp.

---

4. The *Dea Roma* was the city of Rome personified to a goddess.

'Another thing. As Christians were honest in their business dealings, they were losing out to other traders who were more ambivalent about being truthful in business,' said Marcus. 'The Jews and pagans would not trade with them. So, they experienced a level of poverty unlike others in the city.'

'Poverty has often been part of the cost of being a disciple of Jesus,' said Adrian, who thought it was time that he contributed something to the conversation.

'We were also slandered by our Jewish neighbours. They spread false rumours about us, which poisoned minds, as you would expect,' said the bishop. 'But that wasn't all.'

'What more could there be?' asked Max, who really had no idea how difficult things had been for the church in Smyrna all those years ago.

'In the letter, Jesus told us that there were more tribulations to come. We would be imprisoned for our faith in him. Of course, this was also the experience of the apostles. Indeed, it is the possibility for any who followed Christ. So, how were we to respond to all of this persecution?'

Marcus answered. 'Jesus says, be faithful unto death. Be ready to die for my sake.'

'That's right brother,' affirmed the bishop. 'Martyrdom is a real possibility for all who love the Lord. But remember the Lord's promise that enables his people not to be afraid in the face of such violent opposition. I will give you the crown of life, says the Lord, the one who hears will not be hurt by the second death.'

'The second death?' Max was unsure what was meant by that. The other attendants weren't that sure either, but they were happy for Max to be the voice of all the queries.

'The eternal death of hell,' said Polycarp. As a follower of Jesus Christ all his life, Polycarp knew that the Christian life is like a race or a contest. He was well aware that he may lose his life for the sake of his Lord and Master. Yet the promise that Christ gave in his letter to Smyrna filled him with hope. There is a crown of life that Jesus will invest to all who remain faithful to him to the end. Therefore, Polycarp did not fear what was coming at the hands of the enemy. He was determined to keep on following Jesus, no matter what happened to him.

At this point in the conversation, Lucas rose from his seat and went into the kitchen to prepare Marcus something to eat before he set off for the city later in the evening. Marcus returned to his earlier appeal. 'Bishop, will you please consider getting further away from the city? Don't make it easy for the authorities to apprehend you.'

Polycarp shook his head.

'I can see that you will not listen to reason,' he said to his old friend.

'The Lord's will be done,' replied Polycarp.

There was an awkward silence. Adrian thought it a good time to encourage the bishop to rest for an hour.

'I will rest shortly. It would be impolite to leave just as Marcus has arrived,' Polycarp said.

'Do not worry, bishop. I will still be here when you wake,' Marcus assured him. He wanted to spend some time letting the other men know what was happening in Smyrna, without troubling Polycarp with all the details.

Once the bishop had retired for his afternoon siesta, Marcus implored the others to encourage Polycarp to flee for his life. In all his years of attending the many festivals that Smyrna hosted, he had never seen the crowds so agitated and aggressive. The Christians in the city were keeping a low profile while the Games were played.

'Our brothers and sisters in Christ are keeping a very low profile at the moment,' said Marcus.

'That's understandable,' said Adrian. 'The fire of persecution burns brightly in Smyrna.'

'Many have hidden themselves away for fear of being arrested and torn to pieces by wild animals in the arena. I have never known the crowds at the festival to be so vicious against us. They clamour for Polycarp's death. The longer he avoids capture, the fiercer the uproar from the mob. An oppressive atmosphere hangs over the festivities in the city. It is just awful.'

Marcus moved forward in his seat and lowered his voice. 'You men must keep the bishop away from the city. In fact, get as far away from here as you can. I am absolutely sure that Polycarp will not survive if he is caught,' whispered Marcus. He did not want his words to carry to the bishop's ears. Polycarp may be out of sight for the moment, but he was not out of earshot.

'We will do our best to convince him,' said Lucas softly, 'but you know how difficult it is to change his mind. You have seen it for yourself. He is not keen to venture too far away from his flock, especially when they are under attack from ravenous wolves. He is convinced staying close by is the right thing to do. He believes his close proximity brings comfort to other believers in the city. They know that he is not abandoning them.'

'That may well be the case. But the soldiers are on the hunt for him. It will only be a matter of days before they stumble upon this farm. Mark my words, they will stop at nothing until they find our bishop. They have already interrogated some locals to see if they can find out where he is. Only a few elders at the church know he is here,' said Marcus.

'You must do everything you can to keep yourself safe, Marcus,' said Adrian. 'But we are so grateful to you for coming with extra food today. Thank you.'

'It is the least I can do,' replied Marcus.

Kallisto

Polycarp lay motionless on his bed and closed his eyes. But instead of the sweet release of sleep, clear and vibrant images of his childhood came to mind. Polycarp's life had begun as a slave – the property of others to be bought and sold at a whim.

Two well-dressed men walked through the Ephesian gate, one of the entrances into the city of Smyrna. They wore white linen togas embroidered with gold thread. Clearly they were wealthy men. They had an air of superiority about them, not uncommon for slave-traders. The taller of the two men was grasping a young boy's arm to stop him from running away, while the other gentleman scanned the area as if looking for someone. It was a cloudless and bright morning, and the place was bustling with people going about their private business. Suddenly a businesswoman was standing purposefully in their way. One of the slave-traders slowly walked over to her and asked if he could be of service.

'Is the boy for sale?' the lady asked.

The man nodded. 'Yes.' He turned round to face his associate. 'Let the lad come here,' the slave-master said gruffly to his companion. The boy moved timidly towards him. 'This nice lady wants to buy you. What do you say to her?'

'Thank you,' the boy said weakly as he stared at the dry and dusty ground beneath his feet.

'Does the boy have any defects?' she enquired.

'This boy is in perfect order as you can see,' came the reply. 'Just look how straight his back is. No slouching with this one. Strong arms. He'd make a fine servant.'

The lady looked intently at the boy. 'Do you have a name?' she asked.

Silence.

'Speak up boy!' hissed the slave-master.

'Polycarp,' came the quiet response.

'Do you know how old you are?'

Polycarp shrugged his shoulders. 'No.'

'You'll get many years of service from this one,' said the man. 'He's only a nipper.'

'How much do you want for him?' she asked the slave-master.

'Four hundred denarii,' he said. Male slaves usually went for over five hundred denarii, but he could tell that the lady was used to business and would be a tough negotiator. He didn't want to price himself out of the transaction and lose the sale.

The lady was in no mood for haggling. She tossed him a purse filled with coins. 'That will be more than enough,' she said.

He looked inside and his eyes widened with delight. He got more than his asking price. It was obvious that she really wanted the lad in her possession. 'He is all yours,' he said smiling as he withdrew to his associate. 'If only all sales were as easy as that,' he thought.

'Come with me, Polycarp,' she said. As they walked away from the slave-holders, she looked down at him and took his hand. 'My name is Kallisto,' she said. 'I will take good care of you.'

***

Polycarp opened his eyes. He sat up and reached for the goblet of water that was beside his bed. He sipped it slowly. He could hear the muted voices of the men downstairs and, sure enough, Marcus was still there. Perhaps he could rest just a little while longer, he thought. The bishop lay back down and closed his eyes once more. It wasn't long before more memories from his past came flooding back.

***

'I have to take some time away from my responsibilities here,' said Kallisto. 'You will look after my affairs while I am gone, Polycarp.' By now Polycarp had been in her service for a number of years. He had proved himself a good and honest worker during that time. Therefore,

Kallisto promoted Polycarp to be the head servant of her household.

'How long will you be away?' Polycarp asked.

'I am unsure at the moment, but I suspect it will be for a while.'

'When do you leave?'

'Tomorrow at dawn.'

'Are you sure that you would not like me to accompany you on this trip?'

'I need you here. I trust you implicitly. You know that, don't you?'

'Yes. I shall pray for you every day, that the Lord will keep watch over you and bring you home safely.'

'Thank you, Polycarp. I pray for you too and have done so, ever since you came to live with me all those years ago.' Kallisto grasped his hand and Polycarp smiled.

The following day saw Kallisto's departure from Smyrna. Polycarp watched her entourage leave and then immediately took charge of the household. The servants needed encouragement and advice concerning their duties. There was none better to oversee the work than Polycarp.

As time passed, Polycarp proved himself utterly reliable and trustworthy to Kallisto. And it was very important to him that he lived his life in order to please his Lord Jesus Christ in every way. Polycarp could not remember when he first heard about the Lord Jesus Christ. He felt that he had always known him because his parents took him to church every Sunday when he was a young boy. They spoke about Jesus all the time and taught him the Bible. Polycarp and his family were trusting in Jesus. They devoted their lives to Jesus. His father and mother were also slaves. Instead of complaining about the poverty and hardships they faced as servants, they lived and worked to please the Lord Jesus and their earthly masters in whatever they did. And they raised Polycarp to do the same, until he was taken from them.

There was no surprise, therefore, that Polycarp wanted Kallisto to be happy and content too. She had been kind to him since she'd bought him from the slave-traders. She was not like others who owned slaves in the Roman Empire. Kallisto loved the Lord Jesus too. When Polycarp came to live with her, she continued to teach him the Bible. She encouraged him in his faith. Kallisto treated Polycarp like her own son. Watching him grow up was a joy to her. She saw him grow into a man of integrity. He was upright in his dealings with the other members of her household. Just like the God whom he served with his whole heart, mind, soul, and strength Polycarp had no favourites. He treated people the same. He was humble and kind to everyone.

That afternoon, in preparation for the evening meal, Polycarp walked to the storehouses at the edge of Kallisto's grand estate. All sorts of food and drink were kept there, and Polycarp needed to make sure the staff were well looked after. He was accompanied by a small group of widows and orphans. Some poor people from the city tagged along. Polycarp was well known in Smyrna for his generosity to the destitute. Polycarp simply remembered the words of Jesus, give to the one who begs from you and do not refuse the one who would borrow from you.[1] He just wanted to be compassionate, like the Lord Jesus commanded his followers to be.

Polycarp unlocked the storehouse door to reveal a whole array of delicious food and drink, carefully packed and delightful to the senses. Lots of cold pork meat which had been previously boiled in a pot, hung from the ceiling. There were different types of cheese on the shelves. Dotted around the store were pots of honey and jams of various flavours. They sat beside woven baskets that were overflowing with fruit and vegetables. Bottles of sweet wine lined the farthest wall.

'Please, master Polycarp, could I have some corn?' requested a hungry-looking young girl.

'You may,' declared Polycarp, 'and take some cheese too, as you asked so nicely,' he added cheerfully.

'You are always so good to us,' said an elderly widow. 'May God bless you and this household for your kindness, master Polycarp.'

'Take this, and do not worry.' He handed her a small basket that he filled with vegetables and fruit. 'May you know the peace of Christ in your heart,' he said softly. 'Give thanks to God, for he is good. He provides us

---

1. Matthew 5:42 (also read Matthew 25:31-40).

with every good gift from above.'

Polycarp was not aware that his actions were making the other servants in Kallisto's household unhappy.

'He is at it again!' exclaimed the butler. 'I've just seen him walk down to the storehouse and I am sure the crowd following him was bigger than last time.'

'There'll be nothing left for me to cook at this rate,' moaned the cook. 'When is the mistress back?'

'The mistress was vague about that. It could be a few weeks. All she said was that her business was pressing, and that Polycarp was in charge while she's away.'

'You've been in her service much longer than Polycarp,' said the cook. 'I don't know why she didn't ask you to look after things. You are the butler after all.'

'I do not know either. The mistress is very kind to me. But there is no doubt that she loves Polycarp. Since he arrived, the mistress has treated him like her own son.'

'Did he have any parents of his own before he came into the service of the mistress?' asked the cook.

'Yes. He did say in conversation with me a number of years ago that his parents were slaves like us. They were Christians too, like our mistress. He said they took him to church meetings, and they taught him about Jesus of Nazareth. He said there wasn't a day when he did not know Jesus Christ as Saviour and Lord.'

'So how did he end up here?' asked the cook.

'If I remember rightly, their master decided to sell Polycarp when he was a boy. He had no need of him.'

'How awful for Polycarp to be wrenched from his parents like that, at such a young age,' remarked the cook.

'I suppose,' agreed the butler. 'But we all have sad stories like that. I remember the day when …'

'I have to get the dinner ready,' interrupted the cook, and she walked briskly to the kitchen, leaving the butler in mid-sentence. He exhaled loudly and went to finish his chores.

Polycarp sensed a growing frustration from the other servants, but he was undeterred. He continued day after day to give as much as he could from the storehouses of Kallisto, and the people loved him for it. On her return to Smyrna, Kallisto was met not far from her home by the butler, who was deeply distressed.

'What has happened during my absence, that you look so perturbed?' she enquired.

The butler took a deep breath to compose himself, then said, 'You, my lady, had no regard for your servants that were actually born in this house, but instead you placed everything in the hands of this young lad, even though he is a foreigner and came from the East; and he, during your absence from home, plundered everything that there was and left nothing.'

The butler could see that his words angered his owner. He had accused her of unfair favouritism and was implying that she was misguided to rely so much on Polycarp. Yet, she was a successful businesswoman with a canny ability to suss out good or bad characters, or so she thought. Assuming the report was true, Kallisto could not think why Polycarp would betray her trust in this way. She would get to the bottom of it and ask him.

'Polycarp!' she cried out as she entered the atrium. He entered the room genuinely delighted to see her back. 'My lady, it is so good to see you home. May the Lord be praised for keeping you safe.' Kallisto looked angry. 'Whatever is the matter, my lady?' he asked.

'Bring me the keys of the storehouses,' she said sternly.

'Yes, of course, my lady,' he replied, and turned on his heels to fetch them. They walked briskly to the storehouses.

'Open the doors quickly, Polycarp. I want to have a look around,' she snapped.

He opened the doors, and she went inside. Then Polycarp prayed: 'O Lord God, the Father of your beloved Son, that in the presence of your prophet Elijah did fill the vessels of the widow of Zarephath,[2] listen to my prayer, that in the name of Christ they all may be found filled.'

Every shelf was packed with food. Every bottle full of oil and wine. The miracle at Zarephath was repeated in Smyrna! Yet Kallisto was furious. How dare a lowly slave lie to her in such a grotesque way, making her feel bad for trusting Polycarp. Returning to the atrium, she commanded some of her domesticated slaves to beat the accuser and liar. But Polycarp stepped in front of her and stood tall.

---

2. 1 Kings 17:9-16.

'My lady,' he began. 'Please do not ill-treat another for my sake; but rather lay on me the blows intended for him; for he told no lie but deserves praise for his affection towards you. As for me, I did not do this with an evil intent. I only wanted to help the poor. The God and Father of the blessed Jesus Christ has both filled the hungry and has sent his angel to restore to you that which is yours, that you may also have plenty to give to the poor according to the Christian teaching that you follow.'

Polycarp could see fear in her eyes. In all her days, she had never seen such a miracle. He knew what she was thinking – how majestic, how glorious, how fearful is Christ the Lord that he should provide the hungry with good things, and that through me. Polycarp felt exactly the same way.

When Kallisto died, she left Polycarp her fortune and liberated him from slavery. Overnight he became a wealthy man. Although he loved the fact that being well-off enabled him to help the widows and orphans as per the Lord's command, money held no interest for him. His sole desire was to glorify God in his life. He would not let the deadly pursuit of money become an idol in his heart. So he used his blessings and wealth to contribute to the church, enabling gospel ministry.

Over the years Polycarp grew in wisdom and stature amongst the people in the city. He kept the company of those older folks who had seen and heard the Lord Jesus Christ personally. He learned everything he could about Christ from them. Then one day, the apostles came and ordained him bishop in the church at Smyrna. It was an honour that he did not seek for himself. Perhaps his humility endeared him even more to the church? There was no doubt that he had the ability to teach the gospel. He did it all the time. He was a man of great compassion for those lost without Christ. He could speak to young and old alike, and he treated everyone as better than himself.

Now it was his responsibility as bishop to watch over the flock, God's people, in that place. It was up to him to teach the Word of God truthfully, clearly and with passion to all who would listen. Questions that people had about faith, or how they should behave, or about their traditions were all judged by the same rule – was the decision in accordance with the teaching of the apostles?

Polycarp was considered an authority on questions of faith by his flock and peers. This was partly due to his own faith and sound judgement as a man who knew the Scriptures well, and partly due to his personal knowledge of the apostle John. Neighbouring churches wrote letters to him. They asked him advice about troubling issues, and he always replied with words of comfort, encouragement or rebuke if needed. Polycarp never ignored any request for help. His letters were considered to be so wise and profitable for the enrichment of the soul, that they were copied and circulated around Asia Minor.

***

A hand gently touched Polycarp's shoulder. 'Bishop, are you awake?' It was Max.

'I wasn't really sleeping, my boy,' came the reply. 'I was just resting my eyes. Anyway, is it time for me to rise?'

'Yes, Bishop Polycarp,' said Max. 'I think Marcus wants to go soon.'

'Of course,' said Polycarp. 'He will want to get home to his family.'

As he descended the stairs, Marcus greeted him jovially. 'Bishop, you're awake!'

'And you are still here, just as you said.'

'I did not want to leave without saying goodbye.'

'And no doubt you want to impress upon me, once again, the urgent need to get as far away from Smyrna as possible.'

'You know me so well, Bishop Polycarp,' said Marcus.

'I am overwhelmed by the love you and the church have for me, Marcus. Truly, I am. And because I love you all too, I must stay while persecution knocks at our door. I am your pastor. I will not abandon the flock of God while the wolves are circling. Surely you understand?'

Marcus nodded his head, 'yes'. He took the elderly bishop by the arm and led him respectfully to a vacant chair. As Polycarp sat down, Marcus looked at Adrian and Lucas in a way as if to say, can you two not talk

some sense into him? They just shrugged, as if to say,
What can we do? He won't listen to us!

'Despite the danger that you are in, bishop, I can see
that you are not persuaded.' He looked at the dwindling
light outside. 'I must leave now, but if the Lord allows,
I will be back in a couple of days with some more food
and drink.'

Marcus walked to the door and Lucas went with
him. 'And if anything changes for the worse, I will send
word to you,' Marcus whispered to him. 'Do your best
to change his mind.' He looked at the gentle elderly
man in the chair. 'If they find him, they will kill him.'
With those stark words of warning, he left.

Fierce Wolves

The fugitive Polycarp sat in the chair as he watched his friend Marcus leave the hideaway. Adrian began to light some candles around the room. The sun was slowly retreating from view and the men were struggling to see each other in the fading light. Lucas stoked the dying embers of the fire to reinvigorate them. Then he went searching for some more wood to burn.

Polycarp turned to his young attendant to ask for his assistance. 'Pass me my satchel please, Max,' instructed the bishop. It was filled with parchments and scrolls. Due to his quick departure, he only had time to pack those that were particularly dear to him.

'What are you looking for, bishop?' asked Adrian.

'Words of comfort,' replied Polycarp.

He dove into the bag and removed a handful of papers. 'Here, hold these,' he said to Max. Max sneaked a peek at the writings in his hand. He was able to make out that it was a letter, and he got a glimpse of the word Philippi.

'Max stop being so nosy!' chided Adrian.

'What do you mean?' said Max defensively.

'You are not very subtle in your attempts to read things that do not belong to you,' said Adrian.

'What happened in Philippi, bishop?' asked Max, ignoring the rebuke.

Polycarp stopped what he was doing. He looked at Max and removed the parchment from his attendant's hands. It was a letter that he had written many years ago to the church at Philippi in the Roman province of Macedonia. The apostle Paul visited the city when he crossed over into Europe from Asia. The city was given its name by Philip of Macedon, the father of Alexander the Great. The Romans besieged it and gave it the special status of being a Roman colony, which meant that it was like a little piece of Rome abroad.

'Ah, yes … Philippi …,' recalled Polycarp. Max took the liberty of sitting down, even though he had not been invited to do so. Lucas came back with his arms full of wood. He tutted quietly when he saw Max sitting down again.

'They had a presbyter there,' continued Polycarp. 'His name was…was…'

'Valens,' added Adrian.

'Yes, Valens. Thank you, Adrian.'

'The church was in turmoil as I recall. They wrote to me because Valens had embezzled church funds for his own gain. And his wife helped him do it. They had decided to deal sternly with him, but

I wanted to encourage them towards forgiveness and restoration.'

'But he was a thief and a liar,' blurted Max.

'As I said to the Philippians, remember the words of the Master, "forgive and it shall be forgiven to you. Have mercy that you may receive mercy. With what measure you hand out, it shall be measured to you again." The aim of discipline in the church is not to destroy, but to restore, my young Max,' said Polycarp kindly. 'Here, take the letter and read it for yourself.'

Polycarp handed the letter back to Max. The young attendant was eager to find out more and was the first to admit that he was learning much about the gospel and Christian discipleship from Polycarp.

He had heard of Polycarp's patience before he entered his service a few years back. Without a doubt, these attributes enabled Polycarp to build the church in Smyrna into a strong and united body of believers. Polycarp avoided all unnecessary friction with the local authorities in a bid to preserve the Smyrnaean church from persecution during his ministry. Yet, there was one thing that he could not abide, or tolerate – the corruption of the Christian faith by false teachers.

'Listen, Max. When I was made bishop of Smyrna many years ago, I was determined to guard God's people from wickedness and vice by teaching God's Word to them. It was my responsibility to protect the church against false teachers. The apostle Paul called such men fierce wolves[1]. He faced much hardship at the hands of those who blatantly maligned the Scriptures. However, Paul charged all those who pastored God's flock to defend God's Word.'

Whenever the opportunity arose, Polycarp could not help himself launching into teaching mode. He continued. 'First and foremost the Bible is God speaking about God. It is not humanity guessing about God, as some false teachers argue it is. And that means when people try to deny or alter the truth of God's Word, whether they are inside the Church, or outside the Church, the leaders of the Church are to defend the Word of God.'

'Why would people do such a thing?' asked Max. He was completely enthralled listening to Polycarp.

'They will do it because they love power.' Polycarp delivered that word dramatically.

'In their quest for power they will try to divide the Church and draw away disciples after themselves.' He moved forward in his chair. 'Their teaching will be attractive. Their manner will be persuasive. If it were not so, they would not be a danger to the flock. But as the apostle Paul said to Titus, "we must hold firm to the trustworthy Word as taught, to give sound instruction and to rebuke those who contradict it."'[2] In his passion, Polycarp smacked his hand on his knee. He clearly felt very strongly about this.

---

1. Acts 20:29-30.
2. Titus 1:9.

'Bishop, tell him about Cerinthus,' said Lucas. Max was now very intrigued. He wanted to know all about Cerinthus.

'False teachers were troubling the church at Ephesus when John took charge there,' said Polycarp. 'Cerinthus was the most popular among them.'

What was false about his teaching, bishop?' asked Max.

'Well, he was teaching people that the Lord, who gave the Law to Moses in the wilderness, was actually only an angel. Cerinthus believed that God Almighty would have no interest in doing such a thing, because that task wasn't important enough for him to do it himself.'

Max looked astonished by the revelation, but the bishop ploughed on. 'Cerinthus also said that our Lord Jesus was only the son of Joseph and Mary. He was not the Son of God. As far as Cerinthus was concerned, Jesus was an ordinary man upon whom the Holy Spirit fell at his baptism. He also taught that the Holy Spirit left Jesus before his crucifixion in Jerusalem.'

By now the young attendant's mouth was open, flabbergasted by what he was hearing. There was more. 'Cerinthus looked forward to a millennium of feasting and drinking and marrying. His ideas were not the sort of thing to encourage his followers towards sober living,' said Polycarp dryly.

Max's eyes had widened. His surprised facial reactions gave him the most comical expression too. Lucas chuckled.

'As you can imagine, John detested the man's teaching and all his works.'

'I've never heard such a thing,' said Max.

'Well, one day, John entered the public baths in Ephesus. Before he had time to undress, he saw Cerinthus in the changing area. John ran from the bath-house as fast as he could, crying out, "Let us flee, lest even the bath-house fall, because Cerinthus, the enemy of the truth, is within!"'

'This, from a man who would have called down fire upon a Samaritan village and whom our Lord Jesus gave the nickname, "Son of Thunder!"' laughed Adrian. His mirth was infectious, and the others joined in. And, just for a brief moment, the men forgot the reason they were in that abandoned farmhouse.

'You have reacted to deceivers in a similar way to the apostle John, bishop,' said Lucas.

'Have I?' asked Polycarp. 'I do not have any idea to what you are referring,' he added. His tone was light, bordering on impish.

'Remember Marcion?'

'A terrible fellow!' exclaimed Polycarp, throwing his hands into the air.

Max was enjoying the exchange very much, even if the subject matter was very serious. 'So, who was Marcion, and what falsehoods was he spreading about the Lord?' he asked.

'They were many, Max. For one, he rejected the Old Testament as Christian Scripture and said that it was at odds with the New Testament. From that position, I suppose it was not surprising that he ended up concocting two Gods: the God of the Old Testament, full of anger and law and justice, and the God of the New Testament, full of mercy and salvation.'

'But we believe in one God, who is Father, Son and Holy Spirit,' said Max.

'Yes, we do. Marcion also thought that the body and the world around us were somehow inferior, even though the Lord God created the body and the world and said they were good.'

'What did you say to Marcion?' asked Max.

'Marcion came to see me, wanting recognition of his teachings. Naturally I understood them to be severely flawed. They were leading people away from the Lord and the truth of his Word. So, I said to him, "I recognise you; I recognise the first-born of Satan!"'

Max gasped. 'Was that not a bit hard, bishop? How did Marcion react to that?' he asked.

Polycarp moved to the edge of his seat, suggesting that what he was about to say was important. 'Max, we must be zealots for the good. We must keep ourselves from doing wrong and from false teachers and from those who bear the Lord's name in hypocrisy, who lead weak men astray. As John said, "anyone who does not acknowledge that Jesus Christ is come in the flesh is antichrist."[3] Whoever does not acknowledge the testimony of the cross of our Lord Jesus Christ is of

---

3. 2 John 7.

the devil. Whoever perverts the Lord's teachings to satisfy his own desires and says there is neither the resurrection of the body nor judgement to come, he is the first-born of Satan.'[4]

'Yes I understand that, Bishop. But don't the Scriptures encourage us not to malign anyone?'[5] retorted Max.

'When the Scriptures speak of not maligning anyone it means that we are not to be malicious when talking about people. I have never been malicious about anyone in my conversations. However, it does not mean that dangerous people should not be identified and called out, young Max. The apostle John did it when he spoke of Diotrephes who loved to put himself first in everything and wouldn't acknowledge the authority and teaching of the apostles.[6] The apostle Paul spoke of Hymenaeus and Alexander who led many to shipwreck their faith in the Lord Jesus.[7] He also identified Alexander the metalworker and the great harm that he did to him.[8] There were others too. But my point is this, Max. It is very important, as a faithful bishop in Christ's Church, to expose those who are dangerous to the Church. We must be firm when it comes to identifying those who are in fellowship with us in the

---

4. *The Apostolic Fathers Vol III*, edited by J.B. Lightfoot, Letter to the Philippians, Chapter 7.
5. Titus 3:2.
6. 3 John 9.
7. 1 Timothy 1:19-20.
8. 2 Timothy 4:14.

Lord, and those who are hell-bent on the destruction of God's people.' He sat back slowly. 'Some might think that it is maligning someone to do that. But I disagree. I simply do not want anyone who is opposed to the gospel of Jesus influencing you, or Lucas, or Adrian, or Marcus, or any of God's people in Smyrna to their eternal detriment.'

Lucas could see that the conversation was beginning to exhaust the bishop. Polycarp was passionate in his duty to care for the wellbeing of the flock whom God had given him to serve. It was the reason that he refused to go too far away as they were being persecuted by the Romans during the Festival of Hellenes. It was time that he stepped in, he thought.

'Come now, bishop, your point is well made. Shall we take some time to pray for our brothers and sisters back in the city?' he proposed.

'Yes, Lucas, that is a wonderful suggestion,' replied Polycarp. He placed his satchel on the floor and motioned for the other men to gather around him. 'Let us remember, brothers, the promises of our Lord Jesus Christ who said, "where two or three are gathered in my name, there am I among them."'[9] Therefore, in full knowledge of our Master's presence with us, whatever we ask, let us ask in faith without wavering in our minds.'

They bowed their heads and began to pray. The men prayed late into the night. Just for a fleeting moment,

9. Matthew 18:20.

Max lifted his head. Through the atrium roof he saw the glowing white half-moon hanging low in the starry night sky. There were no clouds and it felt very cold. Max bowed his head once more. The little group of believers prayed as sleep started to creep up on each of them. Then exhaustion beckoned them to bed. They agreed to pray again in the morning.

Martyrdom

Smyrna was famous for its magnificence even amongst those who travelled far and wide throughout the Roman Empire and had seen many of the empire's beautiful cities. The streets of Smyrna were adorned with statues of past emperors and famous patrons. Thousands of revellers who had gathered in the city for the Festival of Hellenes admired the great temple built to Tiberius, the second emperor of Rome. They marvelled at the altar to Zeus the Saviour which stood proudly in the marketplace, a most fitting location to remind the local pagans of their false benefactor. The schools of Rhetoric and Medicine gave the city an air of intellectualism. All of it declared Smyrna to be a cultured civilisation and a worthy host of the Games. The local authorities loved the extra boost of cash that the festivities generated for the economy, and for their own pockets. It was their responsibility to provide whatever the mob wanted. But the present demand for Polycarp's death was not yet fulfilled and the proconsul,[1] Statius Quadratus, felt the strain of Polycarp's eluded capture.

'Have you arrested the Christian bishop of Smyrna yet?' The proconsul was seated comfortably in his ornate garden off the atrium of his lavish villa. He was peeling an apple with a small sharp knife when Herod, his chief constable, the commander of the local Roman army cohort, approached. Statius expected an immediate response from the man, and it had better be good news.

'He has fled his home, proconsul, but it won't be long before we find him. He will not have gotten far.'

The proconsul weighed the response carefully. 'In all my years at these Games, I have never seen such lust for blood,' he said, looking intently into the face of his sheriff. 'And the longer it takes to find him, the more incompetent you look, Commander. Rest assured, it will not end well for you, should you fail me.' Statius pointed the knife at his sheriff the commander as he delivered the warning. 'How difficult can it be? He's an octogenarian!' he exclaimed.

'We think that his church has been hiding him. And it doesn't matter how many of them we threaten or beat, they do not give anything away. Knowledge of his whereabouts has only been divulged to a few, and we have not interrogated everyone.'

'The Games end in three days, sheriff. Find Polycarp,' commanded Statius.

---

1. The proconsul was the governor of the province of Asia Minor and ruled the area on behalf of the Roman Emperor.

Herod left subdued yet determined to please his proconsul. 'I will find Polycarp. My men will turn over every stone and look into every crevice in Asia Minor to find this pesky old man, if they have to,' he muttered to himself.

***

Deep down, Polycarp believed that he was going to die soon. He was almost resigned to the fact, in the same way his friend Ignatius, the former Bishop of Antioch, had come to terms with his impending martyrdom about forty-five years earlier. Ignatius had also learned the gospel from the apostle John. He was a little older than Polycarp and over time became his mentor. It was hard for Polycarp not to think of Ignatius in the light of the present persecution of his fellow believers in Smyrna.

It was early and his helpers had not yet arisen from their beds after their focussed and lengthy prayer time the night before. He stood in the farmyard looking out over the countryside. Dawn was breaking, and it gave the hope of another bright yet chilly day. Polycarp was glad of the peace and quiet before the others surfaced. In that precious moment of solitude, his recollection of Ignatius would remain private. It would also give him courage. The summer of A.D. 110 had been savage in its heat, Polycarp remembered. Not the ideal weather to travel in ...

***

A cloud of dust on the road from Ephesus to Smyrna betrayed the whereabouts of the weary travellers. The group were all men, ten in total. At first glance there was nothing overtly remarkable about the way they were dressed, except for the fact that seven of them were church leaders, and three of those were bishops. They were delegates sent from the Christian churches in Ephesus, Magnesia and Tralles to greet Ignatius at Smyrna. He was on his final journey to the arena in Rome, where he was to be brutally executed for his faith in Jesus Christ.

As it happened, Ignatius was nearing Smyrna after his long journey from Antioch. He was accompanied by ten Roman guards, whom he nicknamed his ten leopards, on account of their cruel behaviour towards him.

The two groups merged and continued their voyage towards Polycarp's city. They passed through mountainous country, and in the distance they could see Mount Olympus erect and proud. When they reached the top of the pass, Smyrna was stretched out beneath them, her white temples gleaming beside the blue waters of the gulf. As they neared the city, the traffic became thicker. On that sun-soaked afternoon Ignatius could see the pagan temples all around him. The established order of the Roman Empire seemed unshakable at that time. The east gate of the city was protected by the shrine of Apollo Agyieus, known as the guardian of the highways. To the south near the stadium, stood the Temple of Dionysus, the son of Zeus and nature god associated with ecstatic religious rites. Ignatius looked above to the summit of Mount Pagos and saw the Nemeseion, dedicated to the goddess of revenge. All of these were outside the walls of the city, as was a fine colonnade devoted to the genius of the poet Homer, who was also worshipped there. Even the towers of the city walls were shrines. One was dedicated to the goddess Artemis, the daughter of Zeus and another to her mother, Leto. Others were devoted to Hercules and the Heavenly Twins, Castor and Pollux. It seemed that the walls made a magic circle around the city. But Ignatius did not care for their paganism, and he entered the city without fear.

There was a Christian community at Smyrna and Ignatius knew that Bishop Polycarp would visit him at the earliest possibility. It was extremely likely that representatives from other churches would be there too. The unity of the Church was deeply felt in those early days of persecution. It wasn't long before the weariness of the journey was forgotten in the joy of being welcomed by the brethren.

The days that followed were a lifeblood to the condemned man. Ignatius spoke often with his fellow bishops, most of whom were younger than he. They valued his wisdom and advice based on his years of service of the Master and his church in Antioch. Ignatius did not want to waste the little time he had left. His visit in Smyrna would be shorter than he desired, and there was much to say to his colleagues, especially Polycarp. Ignatius felt that Polycarp was too fond of scholars and secular learning. It made him lenient on the fierce wolves that attacked the sheep of God. He was determined to help his younger colleague to be steadfast and contend for the truth of God's Word unflinchingly. His chance to encourage Polycarp came during an early morning stroll through the city streets, under the watchful eye of his leopards who flanked the men on either side.

'Do you know how long you will be with us, Ignatius?' asked Polycarp.

'I believe it will not be for much longer. I am expected in Rome soon,' he replied.

'I thank the Lord for this opportunity to spend some time with you, my dear brother,' said Polycarp. 'I know the other bishops have greatly benefitted from your advice.'

'That is a great encouragement to me, Polycarp,' said Ignatius. 'I want to pass on some advice to you, if I may be so bold.' Over the short time spent in Smyrna with the small group of his fellow bishops and other leaders from local churches, Ignatius realised that his impending martyrdom in Rome gave him greater authority than he had ever exerted before. He would use it to benefit God's people and help advance the gospel of Christ in Asia Minor.

'You have a love for scholars and secular learning, don't you, Polycarp?' he asked.

'It is good to know current thinking in society, Ignatius. I believe it helps me in my discussions with those who are spreading false ideas about our Lord Jesus. Although, I must admit, their heresies are gaining acceptance among some of my people.'

'You know that those who seek to undermine the truth of the gospel do not come dressed in a heretics uniform with the words "false teacher" inscribed on their foreheads.'

'It would make it easier for our people to spot if they did,' retorted Polycarp.

'They slip in secretly, giving the appearance of being true believers, indeed true pastors. They tell people that God's gospel is all about grace. "God loves you the way you are and therefore you do not need to change one little bit," they say. You have heard it, Polycarp?'

'Yes, I have, Ignatius. Their message is near enough to the truth to deceive and far enough away from it to condemn those who believe it.'

'Quite right, Polycarp. The transforming grace of God and the sovereignty of our Lord Jesus Christ are like twin pillars of the Christian message. By altering these, the good news of the eternal gospel is changed into a poisonous man-centred message that saves no one. I know that you know this, Polycarp. You are a man with a great understanding of the Bible. However, your love for scholarship leads you to argue with these men who only desire to trap you. They make the truth appear less reasonable than their own doctrines.'

'Well then, Ignatius, how do you suggest I deal with them?' he asked.

'I learned not to argue with these false teachers. It was a hard lesson. The only way to bring these pesky fellows into subjection is to stand firm, like an anvil.

Reply to all their blows with an unyielding assertion of the true faith,' said Ignatius.

Polycarp listened respectfully to his elder. After a moment's pause, he changed the subject.

'The other bishops wanted to ask you to write letters of encouragement and edification to take back to their churches. Would you be willing to do that?'

The news caused the elder bishop's smile to light up his whole face. 'With all my heart, Polycarp,' he relied.

With the help of Burrhus, a deacon from the church at Ephesus who acted as his scribe, Ignatius wrote letters to the churches at Ephesus, Philadelphia, Magnesia and to the Trallians. By the end of August, he and his ten leopards left Smyrna for Troas. They were delayed for a time as they waited for a ship to take them on to Neapolis in Greece. When news reached him that the persecution of the church in Antioch had ceased, he took the time to write some more letters, including one to the church at Smyrna and a personal one to his young brother in the Lord, Polycarp.

Ignatius, who is also known as Theophorus,[2] to Polycarp who is the bishop of the church at Smyrna.

It was wonderful to see you face to face. I urge you to graciously press forward on your path to encourage all men that they may be saved. Be gentle in the way that you act towards those who are rebellious against the Lord. Do not let those who teach false doctrine get you down. Again, I say to you, stand firm in

---

2. *Theophorus* means 'the bearer of God'.

the truth of the Lord and be victorious. Continue to look after widows. Do everything in order to honour God. Work hard alongside God's people, struggle together, run together, suffer together, live well together as God's servants. Remember that a Christian is not ruler over his own life but makes time only for God. This is God's work, and it is your work too, so get on with it. I trust in the grace of God that you are ready for a good work that he has prepared for you to do and that will please him in every way. Farewell in the Lord.

***

As he was finishing his letter to Polycarp, news came that his ship was ready to take him to Neapolis in Greece. He sent his letter via messenger to Polycarp, with instructions to make copies and circulate them to the churches that he was unable to visit. From Neapolis, Ignatius and his captors travelled across the Adriatic to Brundusium and up the Via Appia to Rome, which would be his final destination on this earth.

A martyr for the cause of Christ.

The terrible news of the martyrdom of Ignatius in the Colosseum in Rome made its way throughout Asia Minor. Polycarp felt it his duty to inform the church at Smyrna. As the people gathered together, there was the usual hubbub of noise, embraces and laughter. Polycarp took his place and motioned the assembly to sit down. They quietened down as they sat. Polycarp looked sombre. The astute quickly realised that their bishop was about to be the bearer of bad tidings.

'The Lord be with you,' said Polycarp.

'The Lord be with you,' echoed the reply from the congregation. There was a momentary silence.

'Some of you will be aware of the persecution that broke out against the church in Antioch,' he began. 'As a consequence, the Bishop of Antioch, Ignatius, was sentenced to death in Rome. He undertook a long voyage guarded by ten soldiers, from Antioch to Rome. In the summer, he stopped here in Smyrna, and was greatly encouraged by you and other churches from this area.'

As he spoke, some nodded gently as they recalled the gentle bishop who came among them and fortified their faith in Christ on his way to Rome.

'We were deeply saddened by his departure from us. But it is my solemn duty to inform you that the gracious and gentle Ignatius, Bishop of Antioch, our friend, and brother in the Lord, has died a martyr's death in Rome.'

Gasps of shock reverberated around the room. Although they had heard Ignatius was going to be killed, they had prayed earnestly for the Roman authorities to have a change of heart and stay the execution. But this was not the Lord's will. Nor was it the will of Ignatius. He embraced martyrdom for the sake of Christ. 'Permit me to be an imitator of the passion of my God,' he would say to those who would seek a mitigation of his sentence.

Polycarp waited for the sorrowful reactions to subside before saying anything else. Once quiet had been naturally restored, he went on. 'In his Gospel, the apostle John reminds us of the comforting words that Jesus spoke to those who put their trust in him. Our Saviour Christ says, "I am the resurrection and the life. Whoever believes in me, though he die, yet shall he live, and everyone who lives and believes in me shall never die."[3] He was emotional. They could hear it in his voice. So, he paused just for a moment to collect himself, asking the Lord for the strength to continue.

'Ignatius loved the Lord,' he finally said. 'We thank God for his life. But we do not grieve as people without hope. For we believe in the resurrection to eternal life for those who die in Christ. As the apostles testify, Jesus died and rose again, and so we believe that God will bring with Jesus, those who have fallen asleep in him.'[4] His voice had regained its strength. He stood slowly. Polycarp lifted his hands and with authority he proclaimed, 'Christ is risen!'

'Amen!' came the united response from his people and with one melodic voice, they began to sing songs of praise to God.

***

'Is everything okay, Bishop?' The deep voice came from behind Polycarp while he was lost in contemplation. It startled the elderly man. He swung around to see Adrian approaching him from across the farmyard with a concerned countenance.

---

3. John 11:25-26.
4. 1 Thessalonians 4:14.

'Oh, yes, yes,' gasped Polycarp from the exhilaration of the fright. 'You startled me,' he said, beginning to laugh. When he composed himself he added, 'everything is fine, thank you, Adrian.'

'Shall I make you some breakfast, Bishop?'

'That would be lovely. Thank you.'

'Are you coming back in?'

'In a moment, Adrian. I am just enjoying the scene,' he said, as he swept his hand in the air like an artist brushing his hand over a magnificent painting of creation.

Adrian smiled and retreated back into the farmhouse.

A Visit to Rome

Polycarp sat on a broken wall listening to the dawn chorus being sung by the choir of birds all around him in the trees. Adrian was prepping breakfast, and the sound of the other men's voices was audible from his perch. All of a sudden, Polycarp experienced a wave of disbelief coming over him. He couldn't believe how quickly things had changed. Not that long ago he had felt useful for the Lord, but now he was on the run, he felt useless. Compounding his sense of futility were images of an important mission in Rome – a trip of great purpose and importance, not only for Polycarp, but for the churches in Asia Minor.

It had only been a year ago when Polycarp had left Smyrna on the long journey to Rome. Ignatius had done the same journey many years before him but Polycarp had embarked on this journey not for martyrdom's sake, but in the hope of settling a question that was causing friction in the Church. It was not a question of faith, nor of morals, but of custom. There had been a division over when to celebrate the resurrection of Christ at Easter.

Christians in the West followed the example of the apostles Peter and Paul, whom they claimed celebrated the resurrection on the Sunday following the Jewish Passover. Christians in the East claimed to follow the example of the apostle John. They celebrated Christ's great act of redemption on the eve of the Passover, the fourteenth day of the month, whatever day of the week that might be, as it changed each year. It was important to the eighty-five-year-old Polycarp to reach an agreement and end the strife amongst the faithful.

Polycarp took some attendants with him on his quest, including a young Christian disciple called Irenaeus. He was born and bred in Smyrna and known to Polycarp all his life. Like Papias and Polycarp who, as young children, sat at the feet of the apostle John, Irenaeus and his friend Florinus sat at the feet of the wise old Bishop Polycarp and learned the gospel of Jesus from him. Now in his mid-twenties, Irenaeus felt honoured to accompany his pastor to Rome on a very important mission. He was also hoping to gain some pearls of wisdom from him. Everyone in church knew that Polycarp took every opportunity he could to impart his biblical knowledge to those willing to learn. Of course, he did it even when they were not willing to learn – all sorts of people sat in church. But Polycarp wanted to teach God's Word until his dying breath.

The journey was progressing well. About halfway through the trip, Irenaeus noticed that Polycarp and his donkey were struggling to keep up. So, the little group of men took a break and sat under an olive tree to catch their breath. The branches shaded them from the afternoon sun. They used their sacks as cushions to sit on. They rested in silence for a moment, only to have it broken by the inquisitive young man.

'Bishop Polycarp, do you ever get discouraged?' Irenaeus asked. Polycarp thought for a moment.

'Yes, I have felt discouraged on one or two occasions over the years,' he replied. 'Why do you ask?'

'Oh, I don't know,' said Irenaeus. 'I'm feeling a bit discouraged I suppose. We are only halfway there, and my feet and back ache, and I am a third of your age! And I can see that your legs hurt too.'

Polycarp smiled. 'I may be eighty-five years old, but I can keep up with all of you,' he said modestly. Irenaeus and the others laughed.

'Can you tell us about a time when you felt discouraged in your ministry, Bishop?' asked Irenaeus.

Polycarp thought for a moment. Then he said, 'Well, a number of years ago, a group of false teachers were infiltrating some of the local churches with their heresy. They were called the Nicolaitans.'

'I have heard of them,' remarked Irenaeus. 'Didn't the apostle John mention them in his book of Revelation?'

'Yes, he did. The Nicolaitans were a group of people who were trying to work out a compromise with the pagan religions around them. They wanted to make it possible for Christians to take part in some of the pagan religious and social activities in their communities, especially those rituals of the flesh which led to depravity.'

'Didn't Jesus say that he hated the works of the Nicolaitans?' Irenaeus remarked.

'That's right. Our Lord Jesus did say that. The church of Ephesus didn't like them, and the Lord Jesus commended them for that. Sadly, however, the church in Pergamum, just up the coast from us in Smyrna, did tolerate the Nicolaitans. It was very discouraging to hear this,' said Polycarp.

'I've been to Pergamum,' said one of the attendants. 'It's a beautiful place. There were lots of tourists when I was there a few summers ago. Anywhere you go in Pergamum you can see the thousand-foot mountain at the end of the city. It is crowned with temples.'

'The most important temple is to the emperor,' added Polycarp. 'Pergamum was the first city outside Rome to build a temple to worship Caesar as a god. I think it was thirty years or so before the birth of our Lord Jesus. It was their pride and joy. Every year the citizens of Pergamum would go to the temple and burn incense to Caesar. Then they would declare, "Caesar is Lord." Anyone who refused to do it could be arrested and put to death. It happened to a Christian brother in Pergamum called Antipas. He was called to curse Christ. Instead he chose execution.'

Polycarp's last words hung in the air causing a silence to fall over the men. He chose execution. The men wondered how they would personally react if faced with the same dilemma – either recant their faith in Jesus and sacrifice to Caesar, or be faithful to Jesus even if it meant death?

After a moment of reflection, Polycarp went on. 'You must remember, my young brethren, that Satan hates Christian churches. His real focus is our Lord and Saviour Jesus Christ, but Jesus is beyond his grasp. So, he turns his rage on churches. He wants to stop us from shining the light of Jesus Christ into our communities. He will use force and threats against us. He will lie and deceive us with false teaching. He will attack the way we live for Jesus.'

'What do you mean, Bishop?' asked one of the attendants.

'Wrong ideas about God always lead to dishonest behaviour and emptiness,' replied Polycarp. 'We must not conform to the lifestyles of this world. Nor its ways of thinking. Instead, let us be transformed by the renewing of our minds as we hold on to the truth of the Scriptures and contend for the true faith of Christ. Therefore, be on your guard, my dear brothers, because your adversary the devil prowls around like a lion seeking someone to devour. Resist him and stand firm in the faith of our Lord Jesus Christ.'[1]

'The Romans still love to persecute and kill Christians,' said Irenaeus disparagingly.

---

1. 1 Peter 5:8.

'It is nothing personal that we are killed,' said Polycarp. His words were deliberately provocative. He wanted to see how the young Irenaeus would react to this truth.

'It feels very personal to me, Bishop!' exclaimed Irenaeus. The others nodded in agreement but Polycarp fixed his eyes on Irenaeus, his young protégé.

'Remember the words of the Lord Jesus to his disciples shortly before his crucifixion, "If the world hates you, know that it has hated me before it hated you."[2] It is not you that the Romans hate – it is Jesus. And because they hate Jesus, they will kill us.'

Polycarp could see the difficulty this was causing his fellow travellers. However, it was important for them to understand more deeply the cost of being a follower of Jesus.

'I can remember the apostle John speaking of this. The Lord and his apostles were in the upper room the night before his arrest. John said that the Lord was giving them instructions to love one another, and how to cope once he was gone from them. He spoke of the unavoidable hatred that would come to them from the world as disciples of Jesus.'

'I don't understand,' interrupted Irenaeus. 'Why is the world's hatred of us unavoidable?'

'Because the world loves its own kind. It does not love those who do not conform to its ways or thinking,' replied Polycarp. 'Let me ask you a question. Do you like it when people like you?'

---

2. John 15:18.

'Yes. Everyone does, surely?'

'Our society approves of anyone who says the right thing, whether in politics or in religion. If you say the right things, you will be liked. If you do not say them, you will not be liked. It is natural for the world to love its own kind.'

'We all enjoy being in the company of people who like what we say, Bishop, even you,' said Irenaeus.

'Yes, that is true,' admitted the bishop, 'but if you are different to the world, if you are out of step with it, then you will be hated. The world hated the apostles of Jesus because Jesus chose them out of the world. They belonged to him. For their faith in Christ, and their proclamation of the gospel, they were sent to prison, they were stoned with rocks, they were executed in different ways. John spoke often of his brother, James. He was put to the sword for his faith in Jesus. He was killed by people who thought they were serving God, but they were ignorant of God. They did not know God. Those who kill us today are the same. They hate and reject Jesus as Lord and so they kill us because we belong to him, and we proclaim his gospel.'

Irenaeus looked up at the position of the sun in the sky. There were still a few good hours of daylight left.

'I think we should get going again,' he suggested. The men lifted their sacks and put them on their animals. Polycarp climbed up on to the back of his donkey. If such a beast was good enough for his Master to ride into Jerusalem, it was good enough for him to ride into Rome, he thought. His pace was slow and steady. It suited men and beasts alike.

Caesar Augustus and the emperors that followed him gave the city of Rome the most magnificent buildings which any capital ever possessed. The small troop of men, led by Polycarp, marvelled at the magnificent arch that led into the ancient Forum, or marketplace. This was flanked by the temple of Julius Caesar, the Senate house and other arches and temples which rose to the capital on which sat the crown, the Temple of Jupiter.

The vast Colosseum, built by the Emperor Vespasian to seat fifty thousand people, was the home to entertainment and death. It was hard to miss. Polycarp had no love for it, especially as it was the place that his friend Ignatius had been executed for his faith in Christ Jesus. Many others who loved the Lord had lost their lives there.

Their trek through the city to the home of Anicetus, the Bishop of Rome, uncovered several more impressive forums, each with their own imposing buildings. They identified the theatre of Pompey, named after a successful Roman general and statesman who died nearly fifty years before Christ was born. They could see the Baths of Agrippa, and the Pantheon which was a huge building with a colossal dome of concrete dedicated to the gods of Rome. Trajan's Column, composed entirely of marble and surmounted by a bronze statue of the dead emperor, stood as a monument to his victory in the two Dacian campaigns of his reign.

As they travelled through the city streets, Polycarp reflected on the apostle Paul's visit to Athens.[3] It was a marvellous city that was also full of idols. And like Paul, the old bishop felt sick to the stomach at the paganism and idolatry of Rome. As much as he would have liked to speak the gospel of Jesus to the crowds in the marketplace, on this occasion he was singular in focus. The split over the celebration of Christ's resurrection needed to be addressed.

They arrived at the home of Anicetus. They knocked at the house door and were admitted to the vestibule by the door keeper. He led them through the beautifully decorated atrium and into a small sitting room. Opposite was the entrance to a much larger room, probably where the church met each week. Unlike the temples built for pagan worship, Christians usually met in the homes of believers whose accommodation provided rooms large enough to gather in. Through the other end of the atrium, they could see a beautiful garden surrounded by a peristyle.[4] The aromatic smells of garden herbs wafted throughout the lower floor of the house. It was very pleasing to Polycarp and his attendants.

The Bishop of Rome was reclining in the corner of the sitting room reading, until he saw his guests appear. He arose quickly and greeted them amiably.

---

3. Acts 17:16-34.
4. A *peristyle* is a row of columns that surrounds an internal garden or courtyard of a Roman home.

'You must be weary and hungry from your trip,' he said, as he pointed to a white marbled table in the corner of the room, with a small selection of breads, cold meats, cheeses, and fruits of various kinds. Water and wine was also available for the thirsty men. It was a welcome lunch or prandium, as the Romans called it.

'Thank you for your hospitality, Bishop Anicetus,' said Polycarp, sitting on one of the very ornate couches next to his host. 'Yes, we are tired from the journey. I am not as fit as I used to be,' he said cheerily. 'The mind is still fresh, but the body withers and decays.'

Anicetus smiled and said, 'I am very sure there is plenty of life left in you yet, Bishop Polycarp!' Anicetus looked at the men who had shared Polycarp's long journey. Once again pointing to the table in the corner of the room, he said to them, 'Please take whatever food and drink you like. Then come and sit down.'

As the men gathered around the table, Polycarp spoke again to his host. 'I know that we have much to discuss, and I do not want to impose upon you or your household for too long.'

'You are my guests, and I am so honoured to have you here, Bishop Polycarp,' replied Anicetus. 'May I suggest that you and your party rest this evening. We can talk theology tomorrow.'

Anicetus smiled as he got up from his seat and placed his hand warmly on Polycarp's shoulder. It was a welcome suggestion and allowed for the

Quartodecimans[5] to recuperate from their arduous trek across Asia Minor.

'When we were travelling through Rome, I was reminded of the apostle Paul's journey through Athens. It was a city full of idols, just like this one,' continued Polycarp. 'It makes me sick to my stomach looking at them. I am sure you feel the same way.'

'Ah yes. Sadly, there are many idols in Rome,' said Anicetus in a grave tone. 'There is much work to be done for the Lord here. Many people are religious, but they do not know the Lord Jesus for themselves. They put their hope in false gods that demand they try harder to appease them. But whatever the people do, it is never enough. The idols keep them in bondage, enslaved by their religious rituals.'

'It is very serious, Anicetus. Our citizens are always trying to achieve acceptance, success, or greatness. How do they know if they have done enough?'

'They will never do enough,' replied Anicetus. 'It is the nature of false religion to keep people guessing and at enmity with God.'

'And yet, while we were enemies we were reconciled to God by the death of his Son … now that we are reconciled shall we be saved by his life,' said Polycarp, quoting the apostle Paul in his letter to the church of Rome nearly a hundred years previously.

---

5. Christians in the East were called *Quartodecimans* because they celebrated Easter on the fourteenth day of the month.

Anicetus continued the quotation. 'We also rejoice in God through our Lord Jesus Christ, through whom we have now received reconciliation.'[6] Both men smiled at each other.

'Amen, dear brother!' exclaimed Polycarp.

'False religions say achieve,' continued Anicetus.

'But our Lord Jesus says receive,' added Polycarp jovially.

The men knew that the next few days would prove interesting. But Polycarp was glad of a meal and a night's rest before their discussions began.

Early the next morning, before the sun had risen, Polycarp was awoken by the deafening din of the streets and squares. Coppersmiths' hammers blended with the bawling of children at school. It was a common occurrence in the cities of the empire. Nonetheless, the bishop had managed a deep restorative sleep. He would be ready for the day's negotiations in his attempt to end the Paschal Controversy, the name given by the churches to the dispute over when to celebrate Easter.

By late morning, the bishops had retired to a sitting room to start the dialogue. Polycarp took Irenaeus into the room with him. One day the young man would be a church leader. Polycarp and Anicetus both believed it was good for him to see how mature Christians conducted themselves when a disagreement arose. They began with prayer, committing their deliberations to the Lord and asking him for wisdom and unity in the faith.

---

6. Romans 5:10-11.

From the outset of the talks, Irenaeus could see that the two bishops conferred together with the greatest amity.

'We western Christians follow the practice of the apostle Peter and the apostle Paul. So, we have apostolic authority for our custom,' began the Bishop of Rome.

'Well, my dear Anicetus, from my own personal knowledge of the beloved apostle John, we eastern Christians follow the custom derived from him,' said the Bishop of Smyrna. They were both claiming apostolic authority for the custom they each followed.

This could take a while, thought Irenaeus. As far as he was concerned, it didn't really matter when Easter was celebrated. 'The important thing is that Jesus died and rose again,' he thought, 'and not which day it's celebrated on.' Still, he would keep his thoughts to himself, at least for now.

It did not take long for Irenaeus to realise that neither could convince the other. And so the conversation came to an end with a proposal from the Bishop of Rome. 'Although we are of differing opinions on this issue, Polycarp, to show you that we remain in the fellowship of the Holy Spirit, I would deem it a singular honour if you would lead the church in Holy Communion when we gather tomorrow morning in the large room of my home.'

'We have both been eager, as the apostle Paul wrote to the Ephesians, to bear with one another in love, eager to maintain the unity of the Spirit in the bond of peace,'[7] said Polycarp. 'The honour is mine, Anicetus.'

Two days later Polycarp and his companions commenced the lengthy journey home to Smyrna. Although unsuccessful in changing the mind of the Bishop of Rome, Polycarp was pleased nonetheless that they parted company in the love, peace, and unity of Christ. He would bring greetings from the church in Rome back to the church in Smyrna. As he left the Bishop of Rome's residence, Polycarp and Anicetus vowed to pray for each other constantly, until the Lord Jesus take them to their eternal heavenly home.

'There is one Lord,' said Polycarp.

'One faith, one baptism,' added Anicetus.

'One God and Father of all,' continued Polycarp.

'Who is over all and through all and in all,'[8] said Anicetus.

'Amen,' said Polycarp, grasping his friend's hands.

'Goodbye,' added Irenaeus.

Then they left for the long trek home.

---

7. Ephesians 4:2-3.
8. Ephesians 4:5-6.

Good Friends

The wind started to blow a little stronger around the farmyard. Polycarp watched the long grass sway gracefully in the fields all around him. The birds that kept him company so early in the morning were in harmonious song, as if praising their Creator for a marvellous new day. Their melodious sound cheered his heart. It caused Polycarp to be thankful to God for so many wonderful things, such as his mercy and grace to him over his long life. He praised God for his provision of good gifts in his life – for the church family in Smyrna and for Christian friends that encouraged him down through the years. He remembered his friend Papias especially. The last time he saw Papias was a few months ago during the winter of A.D. 155, shortly after his trip to Rome. He was roused from his regular time of afternoon prayer and Bible reading by a loud knock on the front door of his Smyrnaean residence. Max answered it, only to find an elderly man standing in the doorway. Polycarp could hear muffled voices before his young attendant came into the sitting room to announce the unexpected caller.

'Forgive me for interrupting you, Bishop Polycarp, but there is a man here to see you,' said Max apologetically.

'That's okay Max. Who is it?' asked Polycarp.

'He says his name is Papias, and he is the Bishop of Hierapolis,' replied Max. 'He said that apparently you have known him a long time, Bishop.'

Polycarp couldn't believe his ears. His old friend Papias was here to see him! Polycarp sprang up from his chair as if someone had poked him in the back with a long sharp needle.

'Papias!' welcomed Polycarp cheerfully. 'It is so good to see you.' Polycarp embraced Papias like a long-lost brother. 'Please come and sit down next to the fire.'

Papias removed his cloak and handed it to Max, who then left the two men to get reacquainted. 'I am glad to see you, my old friend,' Papias said. The two bishops walked into the sitting room and huddled around the warm grate. Max returned with some light refreshments for the unexpected guest. The bishop always wanted his visitors to receive warm hospitality from him.

'You seem well, Papias,' remarked Polycarp. 'How long has it been?'

'It's been a good number of years since we last saw each other, my friend. You know how it is. Once we get settled into work, it takes over. The next thing we realise is that years have passed, and we have lost touch with friends.'

'Indeed, you are right,' said Polycarp, 'and then when we look at our reflection in the mirror, we see old men staring back at us!' The friends laughed together. 'How are things in Hierapolis?'

'As well as you might expect, Polycarp. There is a lot of work to do. We have nearly one hundred thousand inhabitants in the city, with a large Jewish community. We still experience hostility from many of them and yet some have turned to acknowledge Jesus as the Messiah.

'How wonderful, Papias!' exclaimed Polycarp. He loved to hear such good news from fellow servants of Christ.

'We continue to spread the gospel of Jesus, and though the growth of the Church is slow, we thank God for every sinner who turns back to the Lord. There is much rejoicing in heaven over one sinner who repents.'

'We plant the seed of the Word, and water it, but only God gives the growth, isn't that right, Papias?' Polycarp's question was rhetorical. Papias took some grapes and enjoyed munching them slowly. The fire could be heard crackling in the momentary lull of the conversation. Then Papias said, 'I understand Smyrna is hosting the Festival of Hellenes next year.'

'Yes, that is true,' replied Polycarp. 'The streets of Smyrna will be overflowing with pagans and unbelievers from every part of the province.'

'I am sure the city authorities love the financial boost it brings into the city's coffers,' said Papias, 'not to mention lining their own pockets with gold.'

'It is a lucrative festival for them,' agreed Polycarp. 'I detest the Games, Papias. The killing and maiming and blood. Human or beast. It is barbaric and wrong. The emperor brings death to our cities, and the people love him for it.' Polycarp's gaze drifted upwards, and he uttered an impromptu prayer: 'Sovereign Lord, have mercy upon us, and grant to us your people the boldness to speak out your Word; that people may be born anew in the Spirit; and transferred from the kingdom of darkness into the kingdom of your Son, Jesus Christ.'

Papias bellowed a hearty amen. Another pause.

'When does the festival begin?' he asked.

'February, I think,' answered Polycarp.

'That's only a few months away,' remarked Papias. 'I expect the arrangements are well underway by now.'

'The authorities have begun making preparations,' said Polycarp. 'Buildings are being cleaned, roads are being repaired and the stadium is due a renovation. They are expecting more people to attend this year. So, the plan is to extend the seating in the arena.'

'Sounds like you will have a lot of work to do too, Polycarp. How do you plan to reach the multitudes with the gospel?' asked Papias.

'We will do it prayerfully. Lovingly. Cheerfully.'

'And carefully!' exclaimed Papias. 'It is not uncommon for Christians to be targeted at these events for persecution. It is like a sport for these heathen hordes!'

'They hate what they do not understand,' said Polycarp. 'The populace are ignorant of us. They are easily excitable, and credulous. They see us as atheists who would destroy the world with fire. They think we feast on the bodies of children. They think we are incestuous because we speak of loving each other as brothers and sisters in Christ.'

'There was a mild earthquake in the region of Hierapolis a number of years ago, and the people sought vengeance against us, as if it was our fault!' declared Papias.

'Such nonsense!' Polycarp cried.

Papias shook his head at the memory. 'These sorts of ridiculous accusations against the Church were part of the reason that Emperor Hadrian demanded proper inquiries should be held when there was any public outcry against Christians.'

'Thank the Lord for it too. It gave us a modicum of peace for a while,' said Polycarp.

'It helped that the emperor said that anyone who made false accusations against Christians would be punished severely for doing so.'

'That's one way to discourage mob violence and malicious informers!' exclaimed Polycarp.

'Indeed. I suppose it meant that we were able to be at peace with our heathen neighbours, for the most part,' said Papias.

'Yes, that's true, Papias,' said Polycarp. 'However, we will always be treated with suspicion by the Roman authorities. They think we are a secret society and potentially dangerous. Certainly, that's what Ignatius said in his letters to the churches.'

'Dangerous? How so?' asked Papias.

'From their point of view, we are an organised body under the leadership of a bishop. Each bishop has a number of presbyters with authority from the bishop to conduct worship with Christians in places outside the city.'

'Yes, of course. Christianity is widespread in towns and villages throughout the country,' interjected Papias.

'Exactly. There are deacons who are tasked to care for the widows and the orphans, as well as the sick and those in prison. What alarms the authorities is our unity,' said Polycarp. 'We are members of the body of Christ, whether we live in Ephesus or Hierapolis or Smyrna or Rome or wherever.'

Papias was listening carefully and nodding in agreement. Polycarp went on.

'What completely baffles the authorities is our worship of Christ, especially when we break bread together. By this natural expression of our fellowship, we show how we are united to one another through Christ our Lord. This makes us dangerous because the Romans have always sought to divide and conquer their enemies. However, true believers in Christ are united in him. That's why they kill us when they can get away with it.'

'They cannot kill the Church,' added Papias. 'Jesus said I will build my Church and the gates of hell shall not prevail against it. So, they may take our lives, but that is all they can have. Our souls belong to God.'

'I remember when Ignatius visited us here in Smyrna many years ago,' said Polycarp. 'He was on his way to Rome to be executed because of his faith in Christ Jesus. He said, "It is better for me to be a martyr than a monarch." Well, Papias, if martyrdom is required of us, I hope we can meet it with the same courage and strength as Ignatius did.'

'Let us hope that it does not come to that, my old friend. There are a good few years of life left in you yet,' said Papias, heartily slapping his old friend on the back. 'Tell me, how was your trip to see the Bishop of Rome? Did you manage to persuade Anicetus to celebrate Easter with the rest of us?'

'Unfortunately I was unable to convince him to change his mind. There is no doubt he is a good and faithful servant of the Lord. We talked at length but could not agree. However, as servants of Christ and his people, we remain in fellowship.'

'I am glad to hear that,' said Papias.

'Nothing pleases the devil more than disharmony among the people of God,' said Polycarp. 'He stokes the fire of pride in the human heart and exploits our lust for power and adoration.'

'You can see it in our society too, Polycarp. Everyone is out to make a name for themselves, and the devil stands behind it all,' said Papias.

'That's why we must put on the whole armour of God so that we can stand against the schemes of the devil,'[1] affirmed Polycarp. 'We must stand firm.'

As he was saying these words, Max came and loitered in the doorway of the room. Polycarp liked to take a walk before his evening meal. There was still a bit of daylight left, so he invited Papias to accompany him. Max handed them their cloaks and the men set off through the streets of Smyrna for some exercise. It was a chilly afternoon, but at least it was dry.

'I miss these streets, Polycarp,' said Papias. 'They bring back such good memories of when we were young lads. Do you remember the time when John told us about the morning of the resurrection of Jesus, when he found the tomb empty?'

'He could hardly curtail his joy when he was telling it,' reminisced Polycarp.

'I know. I was mesmerised when he described seeing the stone no longer covering the entrance to the tomb, and the grave clothes just lying there,' said Papias.

'Then he said death had been conquered that day,' added Polycarp, 'and now nothing can separate us from the love of God.'

'We must hold on to this truth, Polycarp,' said Papias. 'We cannot be separated from God's love for us in Christ.' As he walked beside his friend, Papias raised his right hand and pointed to the pagan religious edifices that lined the streets of the city. 'Not our enemies, nor

---

1. Ephesians 6:11.

persecutions, nor sufferings, nor tribulations can take us away from the Lord who loves us.'

Polycarp knew what his friend was trying to say. Although Christians may experience persecution and intimidation at the hands of their enemies, God's love for them remains sure and steadfast. Polycarp remembered the wonderful promise of the Lord Jesus to his followers; 'I am with you always to the end of the age.'[2] The Lord's constant presence always comforted Polycarp in his ministry.

'Thank you, my friend,' said Polycarp. 'How true your words are. It is good to be reminded of them.'

Their walk had been reduced to a meander, as they passed the public library. The daylight was beginning to fade, so they decided to head back to Polycarp's home. The conversation, however, was not dwindling. Even after many years apart, friends always manage to pick up a conversation where they left off.

It was not long before Polycarp's front door was upon them. Polycarp turned to face Papias. 'Will you stay for dinner?' he asked.

'I would love to, my old friend,' came the heartfelt reply.

Max quickly opened the door. Lucas and Adrian had spent the afternoon preparing and cooking the evening meal, as the bishops strolled around the streets of Smyrna. The pleasant aroma of cooked chicken greeted them on entry into the atrium. They moved

---

2. Matthew 28:20.

to a table and sat down, in excited anticipation of the feast that was being set before them. Polycarp asked his friend to say grace, who willingly praised God for all his goodness and mercy to them in the provision of such a fine spread. He kept his prayer short because he didn't want his dinner to get cold. The conversation turned to new converts.

'What do you do with people coming from one of these pagan religions who then profess faith in Christ?' asked Papias.

'Well, our Lord Jesus Christ does not tell us just to make new converts, but to make disciples. So, I spend time with them as they begin a new way of life following Jesus.'

'What do you talk about when you spend time with them?' asked Papias. His questions were coming thick and fast.

'I encourage them to kill,' said Polycarp in an understated way.

'Kill?! Who? The Romans?!' exclaimed Papias roguishly.

'Yes, I encourage them to be murderers, but not the Romans,' chuckled Polycarp. 'I tell them they are to put to death the earthly nature. They are to kill it off. They are to put off the old self and put on the new,' he said.

'Say "no" to the world and "yes" to Jesus,' added Papias.

'That's right. Now that they are in Christ, it makes no sense at all to go on living for themselves and

ignoring Jesus. They are to live for the world to come,'
said Polycarp. 'As Christians, we put into practice
what we believe. We put off the old way that we used
to live, with all the practices that came with it. It's
very interesting. We put off all the things that come
naturally to us.'

'You are talking about what the apostle Paul said in
his Colossian letter,[3] aren't you, Polycarp?'

'I am indeed. You recall what the apostle Paul said,
Papias: "put to death ... sexual immorality, impurity,
indecency, lust, evil desires and greed which is a form
of idolatry."'

'You might be an old man like me, Polycarp, but
you still have a great memory for the Scriptures!'
bellowed Papias.

'It is something I give thanks for every day, Papias.
Anyway, Paul said, "you must put all these things away:
anger, wrath, malice, slander, and obscene talk from
your mouth." Also, "do not lie to one another."'

'That is quite a list. You are absolutely right, all
these things are natural to every person,' agreed Papias.
'Parents never have to teach their children to be greedy.
In fact, it's the opposite, isn't it? They must be taught
how to share.'

'It is the same with lies,' interrupted Polycarp. 'They
are generated from our own hearts.'

'Anger, too,' said Papias. 'People do not need to be
taught how to lose their temper. They just do it.'

---

3. Colossians 3:1-17.

'Well, I tell every new believer that these things bring the wrath of God. Jesus Christ died on the cross because of these things. So, these things must be killed,' said Polycarp theatrically. 'We must put to death the old self with its lies and anger and bad language and all the rest. These things are antisocial. That is the character of sin. It always destroys relationships.'

'I assume you move on to the positive side of things,' said Papias.

'Of course,' affirmed Polycarp. 'So, I tell them that because we are God's chosen people and because we have been rescued out of darkness and into the kingdom of God's beloved Son Jesus, we are therefore to put on righteousness, love, forgiveness, kindness, humility, gentleness and patience.'

'It is a very similar list to the fruit of the Spirit that Paul speaks of in his letter to the Galatian Church,' said Papias.

Polycarp agreed. 'Tell me, Papias, who would you want living next door to you? The person who is filled with anger and rage, and malice and slander, who has a foul mouth and tells lies, or someone who is filled with the love of Christ, forgiving and kind, humble and gentle of heart, and who is patient?'

'That's a great question,' declared Papias. 'Who doesn't want someone with Christian characteristics living next to them?'

'As Christians, there is the new nature of heaven to put on,' said Polycarp, 'and love will bind God's people together. When we come into fellowship with God, we take on his family. The way that we can get on with each other is by loving one another and by showing gentleness and kindness to each other.'

'It's the outworking of the new relationship with Jesus as Saviour and Lord,' said Papias.

'That's what I tell new converts,' said Polycarp. 'Kill the old! Put on the new.'

'Thrilling! I am so glad I asked,' smiled Papias.

This was the last time the two old friends shared a meal and a conversation together.

***

Polycarp was deep in thought. As he fondly reminisced about Irenaeus, Anicetus and Papias, he was totally unaware of Max walking towards him from behind.

'Bishop Polycarp,' he said softly as he approached, but there was no response. Max raised his voice slightly. 'Bishop Polycarp.' This was enough to jolt Polycarp back into the present. He stood up from the wall and turned to his young attendant.

'Yes, Max, what can I do for you?' he said kindly.

'Adrian sent me to fetch you for some breakfast, Bishop. He thinks you've had enough fresh air for the time being.'

Polycarp laughed, believing that Max was probably not meant to add that little bit to the message from Adrian.

'I am quite peckish now,' admitted Polycarp as he walked with his young helper to the entrance of the hideaway. 'Let's get something to eat.'

The Escape Plan

The visit from Marcus left the men feeling uneasy about their present location. Perhaps it wasn't a good idea to stay too long in one spot. After all, it is harder to hunt a moving target. Adrian and Lucas were huddled in a corner of the atrium, devising a plan of action to keep Polycarp safe. It would need to be presented as a suggestion, as Polycarp did not take kindly to orders concerning his wellbeing. It was difficult enough getting him to the present safe haven, as he did not want to leave his people and go too far from them.

The men knew of another vacant farm close by that would provide sanctuary from the Roman hunters. They hoped and prayed that when the festival was over, the killing spree would end and allow them to go home. In the meantime they would do everything they could to keep Polycarp safe and well.

After his early breakfast, which Adrian had so wonderfully prepared, the bishop retired to his room. He wanted to spend some time reading the Scriptures and praying for his people and for peace in Smyrna.

Later that morning, as he descended the stairs and entered the atrium, he saw his attendants in deep, whispered conversation. When the bishop approached them, the men broke off their conversation. Lucas was concerned when he saw Polycarp. Beads of sweat were visible on the bishop's brow. He asked, 'are you feeling alright, Bishop?' As it was February, Lucas knew that Polycarp's sweltered appearance wasn't from the heat. He walked quickly to the bishop and helped him into a chair. Polycarp seemed perturbed.

'Thank you, Lucas,' said Polycarp. Lucas knelt beside him. Turning to his colleague he said, 'Adrian, fetch the bishop some water, please.' Then he turned back to Polycarp. 'What is the matter, Bishop?'

Polycarp looked directly at him and said, 'I was kneeling by my bed, in earnest prayer. I was pleading for the killing to stop. I was praying for our enemies, that they might repent and turn to Christ. Then I fell into a deep trance.'

Adrian arrived with a goblet of water from the kitchen. He handed it to Polycarp, who took it with both hands and drank deeply from it. Polycarp caught his breath and continued. 'I fell into a deep trance, Lucas. I saw the pillow on my bed burst into flames. They grew higher and higher. And now I know, Lucas, I know.'

'What do you know, Bishop?' asked Lucas softly.

'I know how I must die,' replied Polycarp. 'Don't you understand? The Lord has shown me.'

Lucas turned and looked at Adrian. 'How must you die, if you must die at all?' asked Adrian.

'I must be burnt alive,' said Polycarp.

His words hung in the air like a cloud on a windless summer's day. The two men were simply stunned. They had no immediate reply. They just looked at each other. Then they looked at the bishop, who in turn was looking at both of them. They really did not want Polycarp to die. The church at Smyrna wanted their bishop to be around for a good while yet. That's why they were hiding him! Although he was eighty-six years old, mentally and physically he was still a very able man. More than that, though, he was their beloved pastor. He had taught them the Scriptures faithfully and clearly for decades. His love for Christ was absolute. His love for the church was sincere. He was a man who ministered publicly and privately day and night, utterly committed to reaching the population of Smyrna with the gospel of Jesus Christ. His godliness was transparent. Everybody saw how he lived among them. He believed what he preached, and he lived his life accordingly. But now he was telling them that he was going to die a most horrific and painful death by fire. It was all very hard to take in.

Lucas broke the silence and said, 'Let's hope it is not for a good while yet, Bishop. We like having you around.'

'Do not be flippant, Lucas,' rebuked the bishop. 'The Lord's will be done.' And with those words, he got up and walked out of the sitting room. The men were shocked at Polycarp's sudden exit. They just looked at each other in stunned silence.

Then Adrian spoke. 'It might not be a good moment to suggest a change of hideout.'

'I think you're right,' said Lucas as he stood from his crouching position next to the bishop's chair.

Polycarp found Max and the other two lads in the kitchen preparing lunch.

'Have you seen my satchel, Max?'

'Yes, Bishop, you brought it upstairs with you last night after Marcus left,' he replied. 'I can have one of the boys get it for you if you want?'

'Thank you, Max. No, it's okay. I shall get it,' said Polycarp. 'Yes, I remember now. I put it under my bed.'

Polycarp climbed the stairs to his makeshift bedroom and found the satchel exactly where he left it. He sat on the bed and heaved it onto his knees. It was filled with papers. He pulled them out and began skimming the first paragraph of each one. It wasn't long before his eyes rested on the letter he was searching for. It was old, creased and worn because Polycarp had read it over and over again. It encouraged him in difficult days, and it began: Ignatius, who is also known as Theophorus, to Polycarp who is the bishop of the church at Smyrna. It was wonderful to see you face to face …

When Polycarp received that letter from Ignatius forty-six years previously, he promised himself that he would try to follow the wise and godly advice contained within it. But like the apostle Paul, he couldn't help but feel that his race was now finished, especially having seen his fiery demise from the Lord in prayer. Over his many years of ministry in Smyrna, he had fought the good fight and kept the faith. All that remained was the prize – the crown of righteousness given to those who love the Master.[1]

He clutched the letter from Ignatius to his chest and prayed for strength to meet his end with dignity and courage. O that the Lord would grant me a moment to speak the glorious gospel of Christ to my tormentor, he thought, I would take it!

It wasn't long before Polycarp was beckoned below for some food. Max and his two young helpers had finished preparing lunch of the usual cold meats, along with some grapes, tomatoes, and cheese. There was water to drink as well. Polycarp said grace, and the men helped themselves. They were hungry and kept their rations small to help stretch out the supply for a few more days.

As they were eating, Adrian and Lucas thought it the right moment to put their relocation plan into action.

'Bishop, we have been here a few days,' said Adrian.

'Maybe it is time to choose another place to stay,' suggested Lucas. 'We do not want to make it easy for the soldiers to find us.'

'Surely we are well hidden,' Polycarp replied.

---

1. 2 Timothy 4:7-8.

'For the moment, yes. They would have found us by now if we weren't,' said Lucas, 'but I feel the longer we remain in one place, the quicker they will find us. Do you not agree, Bishop?'

'Perhaps you are right,' conceded Polycarp. 'Is there anywhere else we can go?'

'I know of another place,' said Adrian. 'It is a deserted farm, like this one. It is not too far from here.'

'But far enough to make capture all the more elusive,' interjected Lucas.

'If you are agreeable, Bishop, Max and I can travel to it tomorrow to make sure that it is safe for us,' suggested Adrian.

'We should be ready to leave the day after that, if all is well,' said Lucas.

Polycarp thought for a moment. 'Lucas and the others will remain here with me while you go scouting?'

'I will be right here by your side, Bishop,' reassured Lucas.

'As always,' added Polycarp.

'As always, Bishop,' said Lucas.

***

The two men left the farm early the next morning before the sun came up. They packed some food supplies to keep them going throughout the day. It was easier to travel on foot, although it made for slow progress through the countryside. Max was constantly looking over his shoulder to make sure that no one was following them. Slowly the sun peeked over the horizon to announce a fresh new day. It was cold but at least it wasn't raining. The men were thankful for that. After a few hours of watchful travelling, they approached a thoroughfare that heightened their agitation. A short distance ahead, Adrian spotted a donkey and cart crawling along the stony road. He noticed two men in the cart. One was driving and the other seemed to be napping because his head was bowed, and his chin was tucked tightly against his neck. 'Get down,' he whispered to Max. They ducked behind a group of hefty misshapen boulders just off their path. The driver stopped the cart and turned his head to look in their direction. He didn't see them, but he didn't move off either. Thieves and robbers were always a threat to any traveller, especially when there would be no witnesses to their crime. The fugitives, however, were well hidden behind the large rocks. Max didn't realise that he was holding his breath.

Satisfied that the coast was clear, the driver and donkey headed off again. As the cart trundled further down the road, Adrian turned to his younger companion and said, 'You can breathe now.'

Max exhaled quietly. 'That was close,' he said.

'Come on. We're not too far away,' said Adrian.

Cautiously they emerged from their hiding place and walked to the track. There was no sign of anyone else. They hurried across it and kept going until hunger got the better of them, forcing a break in the journey. They found a suitably large tree and sat down to eat.

'When we get to the farm, we need to make sure that it is completely deserted,' said Adrian.

'You mean, check for squatters?'

'Yes. And we should stay for a while to see if anyone travels too close to it. It would be disastrous if our presence there drew unwanted attention from passers-by. If all goes well, we can get back to the bishop this evening with good news.'

'And if all goes well, it will be an early start again tomorrow.' Like many young people, Max found early mornings hard.

'You know the bishop rises early to pray. We'll leave when he is finished. Now, eat quickly. I want to get going.'

Within the hour, the two men stealthily advanced on the abandoned farmhouse. From its appearance, the farm had been empty for a number of years. Although there were holes in the roof of the house, there was enough unbroken roof to provide adequate shelter, at least for a few more days. Inside it was cold and dusty in some rooms, while others were damp and overgrown with vegetation.

The farm was off the beaten track, but the men remained there for a few hours to ensure its isolation provided the perfect hideaway. They saw no one. Content with its remoteness, they started off on the trek back to the bishop to tell him about his new short-term lodgings.

***

Polycarp spent the day on his knees praying for his helpers; for his enemies; for those in authority; for the churches of Asia Minor; for peace to rule the hearts and minds of the people; for all to come to know, love and serve the Prince of Peace. He hoped the news from the two-man exploration team would be favourable. When Adrian and Max returned, the bishop embraced them. They could hear the relief in his voice.

'Thank the Lord that you have returned safely,' said Polycarp. 'All day I have been praying that the Lord would bring you back to us in one piece.'

'It was a good journey,' replied Adrian, 'and the farm is perfect for us. It is abandoned and remote.'

'We can stay there for a few days, then reassess things, Bishop,' said Lucas positively.

'Did you see anyone?'

'Only a couple of people, but they didn't see us,' said Max. 'If we set off early in the morning, we shouldn't have any problems getting there undetected, Bishop.'

The men spoke with confidence. Polycarp felt reassured. 'Then we shall depart in the morning,' he declared.

They mustered what little sleep they could, but no one rested well that night. The morning could not come quickly enough for Polycarp. As was his custom, he arose and knelt by his bed to pray. He heard the noise of the others gathering their few possessions together. When he joined them downstairs it was still dark, except for a couple of candles giving off enough light to guide their way around the furniture in the room.

Lucas was giving instructions to the young helpers, explaining where they were going. They were to remain behind and let Marcus know where they were headed. They were expecting him to come to the farm later that day with some more food supplies. 'Tell him where we are, and bring him to us,' said Lucas. 'Keep off the roads and guard your backs,' he added. The boys understood and nodded, 'yes'.

'It's time to go, Bishop,' said Adrian and extinguished the candles. 'Remember, sound carries farther in the darkness, so try to be as quiet as possible.'

Max led the way out of the farmhouse and helped the elderly Polycarp on to his donkey. Once he was happy that the bishop was securely mounted, they moved out. The two boys stood at the doorway and watched the little group of refugees walk away. Moments later, they were out of sight. The boys went back inside to wait for Marcus.

***

Polycarp and his companions had left the farmhouse in the nick of time. The search party reached the edge of the farm that afternoon. 'Remember, we are only interested in Polycarp,' said the centurion who was in charge of the search party. 'Secure the others in case they get feisty and try to protect him. But being Christians, I suspect there will be little resistance.' He almost sounded disappointed when he said that. All of Rome knew that Christians were not violent people.

They dismounted their horses and split into two teams. As they advanced, one team went around to the rear of the farm in case anyone tried to slip out the back. The other furtively approached the front. The two boys were inside playing nuts[2] on the atrium floor. They were so focussed on their game that they were completely oblivious to the impending danger from the encroaching Roman soldiers.

Suddenly two soldiers rushed in from the front doorway and grabbed each of the boys by the scruff of the neck. They tried to pull away from their captors, but the soldiers' grips were too strong. The boys were forced to sit down, and their hands were tied behind their backs. The centurion was in no mood for any shenanigans. He had been hunting Polycarp for a while and his patience had well and truly run out.

'Where is Polycarp?' he asked them. One lad whimpered. The other said nothing. The centurion did not have time for silence. He gave the nod and both boys were beaten repeatedly until one of them could not hold out any longer. He disclosed the new whereabouts of Polycarp and his attendants. He just wanted the beating and the pain to stop. The centurion gave the order to release them both from their bonds. His intention now was to bring the informant with him and bag his prize. They pushed him forcefully out of the farmhouse to where the horses were grazing. He looked over his shoulder and saw his friend slumped

---

2. The ancient equivalent of marbles.

over in his chair. Thankfully the lad was alive, although badly hurt. He was sure that Marcus would tend to his beaten friend once he arrived later on.

It was Friday afternoon when the soldiers left the farmhouse with their informant. They were not familiar with the area surrounding the city of Smyrna and relied on the boy to lead them. It was late in the evening when they drew near to the farm where Polycarp and the other men were hiding. The boy was warned not to give away their advance, or else he would be killed where he stood. He did not need to be told twice. Not a peep was heard from his lips.

Lucas was keeping watch from a window when he saw the moonlit outline of the hunters drawing near. He turned quickly and whispered loudly, 'Adrian. Max. There are soldiers approaching. We have to go!'

Polycarp was resting upstairs. Max bounded into the room and hastily relayed the terrible news to his bishop. 'We need to leave now, Bishop. They are very close!' he whispered excitably. He heard the bishop's sharp intake of breath. Polycarp breathed out slowly. Quietly and calmly he said, 'I am not running anymore, Max. May the will of God be done. Go and tell the others.' Max obeyed his elder. Fear gripped the men as the soldiers entered the building.

The centurion squared up to Lucas and gave him a hard stare. 'Where is Polycarp, the so-called Bishop of Smyrna?' he demanded. Before Lucas said anything, Polycarp came down the stairs and stood before them.

'Greetings, centurion,' said Polycarp. As he walked to his chief captor, he looked at the rugged faces of the exhausted men who had been hunting him down. 'Your men look hungry and in need of rest,' he remarked.

'My men are fine,' came the aggressive reply.

'Come now, centurion. Allow my men to prepare something for all of you.' He turned to his three devoted helpers and asked them to make a plentiful supper for their guests. They disappeared into the kitchen to cook for the soldiers.

'Do not worry. They will not run away while I am here. And I am too old to outrun any of you!' The centurion's demeanour softened noticeably. A fire was burning in the grate and Polycarp fed it with some wood from a pile next to the hearth.

'Please, men, sit down and rest while supper is prepared for you.' Polycarp motioned to the soldiers who immediately looked at their commander. He nodded affirmatively and they found somewhere in the room to take the weight off their feet.

Another soldier entered the room. He was holding the young informant tightly by the arm. The boy's face was bloodied and bruised from the beating he received that afternoon. Seeing his comrades relaxing in the room, the soldier released his grip. Polycarp took the boy by the shoulders and guided him into the kitchen. The lad started to weep. Max rushed over to help.

'I am so, so sorry, Bishop,' sobbed the boy as he looked into the kindly face of Polycarp. 'They wouldn't stop hitting us.'

'Is he alive?' enquired Max of the other boy.

'Yes, I think so.'

'I'm sure Marcus is tending to him even now as we speak,' said Max reassuringly.

Polycarp gently handed the boy over to Max and said, 'tend to his wounds and feed him.' Max nodded. The bishop turned and joined his captors in the other room.

'Your supper is nearly ready,' reported Polycarp as he entered the room. 'May I have some time to pray, commander?'

'If you must.'

Polycarp moved to a far corner of the room, still within view of the soldiers. He got down on to his knees and began to pray sincerely for them, and for their leaders in Rome. The men could hear every word. No one had ever prayed for them before. Polycarp continued to pray for the church in Smyrna and in the world, begging the Lord that they would be faithful in the midst of persecution to hold out the Word of Life to a dying world. As he prayed, Adrian and Lucas appeared with supper. They did not disturb the bishop, but continued to serve their guests, as Polycarp called them.

An hour later, Polycarp concluded his prayers and joined the others for something to eat. It was now very late, and the centurion did not cherish the thought of transporting a prisoner back to the city in the dead of night. He decided to wait till the morning and leave with Polycarp at first light. The soldiers took it in turn to rest while others watched over Polycarp and his attendants to make sure they didn't escape. They did not know that Polycarp had no intention of fleeing. He knew full well that his time serving the Lord was nearly over. He was ready to die.

Faithful unto Death

It was nearly noon on the Saturday morning in February
A.D.156 when the party reached the gates of Smyrna.
It was a cold, windy day in the city. They were met
by Herod, the commander of the local Roman army
cohort, and his father, who was called Nicetes. They
sat in a grand carriage that denoted the high status of
the occupants. They were not alone. Some hard men
stood guard over them. Herod was always escorted
for his own protection, because not everyone thought
the Roman occupation in Asia Minor was a good thing.

Polycarp was perched on the back of a donkey as he
rode to the gate. The soldiers surrounded him to dispel
any attempt of escape. It amused the bishop slightly, as
he knew his little donkey could not outrun the mighty
steeds of his captors.

Herod smiled as he saw the bishop approaching. 'We
have him,' he said to his father.

'The proconsul will be pleased,' replied Nicetes.
'This old man gave you the run-around. You were
beginning to look incompetent.'

'Subtle as ever, father,' said Herod. 'Polycarp was never getting away from me. And here is the proof,' he said, pointing to the soldiers.

The horses came to a standstill beside the carriage. The centurion reported the success of the hunt and presented the captured fugitive to Herod.

'Well done, centurion,' said Herod. 'I trust there were no difficulties in his capture.'

'None, sir,' replied the centurion. 'He was very compliant.'

'Good, good,' said Herod. Turning to Polycarp he said, 'I am sure you are tired from your journey. Your ride doesn't look very comfortable. Please join me and my father in my carriage. I insist.' His tone was amicable, but Polycarp believed his motives were sinister. It was an offer that Polycarp could not refuse, even though he wanted to. He dismounted his donkey and climbed on board the carriage. It trundled slowly past the temples and statues of the city on course for the stadium. The soldiers accompanied the carriage into the city just in case some of Polycarp's supporters should attempt to free him. Polycarp sat quietly in the company of his antagonists. The interrogation began gently.

'I believe you are a bishop,' said Nicetes politely.

'Yes,' replied Polycarp.

'Please forgive my ignorance, Polycarp, may I call you Polycarp?' asked Nicetes.

'Yes,' said Polycarp.

'What is a bishop?' asked Nicetes.

'A servant of Christ Jesus,' replied Polycarp.

'Yes, I have heard of this Christ.' Nicetes then looked at his son. 'Your aunt followed this Christ of his. Silly woman,' he said, waving his hand dismissively. Herod appeared impatient with his father's line of questioning. Polycarp marvelled at the power of the gospel to save anyone, even a member of Herod's family. He praised God for his grace to humanity, that anyone who calls on the name of the Lord Jesus shall be saved.

'You would do well to follow her example,' said Polycarp. 'Call upon the one true Lord for salvation. Bow the knee to Christ Jesus. Repent of your sins and follow him,' said Polycarp.

Herod was incensed. 'Stop all this nonsense, Polycarp!' he said forcefully. 'There are many lords. Just look around you.' The numerous pagan temples of the city could be seen along the road to the stadium. Herod's outburst indicated a passion of belief, even if it was wrong belief. Herod's eyes were filled with hate. Polycarp believed that when people reacted to the gospel with hatred, it didn't mean that they cared very much about their beliefs, but they just disagreed strongly . Of course, the Christians in Smyrna found it more hurtful to face angry opposition. It could literally cost them their lives. Yet in all his years of evangelism in Smyrna, Polycarp always found it less hopeful if the gospel was met with apathy, although it was much less painful. It was harder to talk about the gospel with someone who just didn't care if it was true or not. It just didn't matter to them. Those conversations saddened Polycarp deeply and usually did not last long.

Polycarp remained calm and composed. He said nothing in response to Herod's words. This annoyed Herod and Nicetes all the more.

But Nicetes used a tone that was soft and yielding in an attempt to ease the tension. 'Now, what harm is there in saying, "Lord Caesar" and in offering incense, and so on, and thus saving yourself?' Polycarp made no reply.

'Come now, Polycarp. You're an intelligent man. What do you say?'

Polycarp turned his gaze out the carriage window and remained quiet.

'Such impertinence,' spat Herod. 'Do you not know who I am?'

Nicetes put his hand on his son's arm as if to say, calm down.

'Surely there is no harm in saying that "Caesar is Lord" and offering incense to save your own life, Polycarp,' repeated Nicetes.

'I would advise you to do it, if you want to live,' added Herod, pointing his fat left forefinger at the bishop.

Without hesitation, Polycarp replied, 'I do not intend to do as you advise.' His clear response and quiet demeanour only angered the interrogators further.

Polycarp was not going to recant his faith in Christ and worship Caesar.

The carriage pulled up to the gate of the stadium and stopped brusquely. 'Let us see if the proconsul can change your stubborn mind,' said Herod through gritted teeth. 'Get out!' he shouted. Father and son pushed Polycarp so roughly from the carriage that the old bishop grazed his shin. Immediately he was encircled by guards. Paying no heed to the pain of his leg, he walked straight on, into the stadium. On seeing him enter the arena, the crowd sent up a deafening shout of 'Polycarp! Polycarp!' The stadium was in a tumult.

Polycarp looked up to the rows of spectators who had gathered for the day's sport of the Festival of Hellenes. Thousands of people watched with wicked glee as the old man was led in front of the proconsul, Statius Quadratus. They had eagerly awaited his trial and now Polycarp stood in front of them, charged with being a Christian, a crime punishable by death. Some of the church family had crept into the stadium when the news reached them that Polycarp had been brought there. As they snuck in to see their beloved bishop for the last time, they were deafened by the devilish din of the degenerate hoard. Then stillness came over the gathered mass as they strained their ears to hear the usual form of examination at these trials.

'What is your name?' asked the proconsul.

'My name is Polycarp,' he answered.

'Polycarp. Are you a Christian, Polycarp?' The proconsul was straight to the point. It seemed that he was in no mood to play with his catch.

'Yes. I am a Christian,' replied Polycarp.

'They say that you are the Bishop of Smyrna, is that so?'

'Yes.'

'You look after the Christian church here?'

'I am their overseer. Yes.'

'You are an elderly man, Polycarp. How old are you?

'I am eighty-six years old.'

The proconsul paused for a moment before the persuasion came. In the hush, a voice could be heard crying out from the crowd, 'Kill Polycarp!' It sparked a momentary escalation of violent outbursts towards the bishop, then it settled again.

'Polycarp. Have respect for your age,' said the proconsul. 'Swear by the genius of Caesar. Repent! Say, "away with the atheists."' Polycarp found the term atheists a most disagreeable and inaccurate word to describe Christians. They believed in the one true and living God of the Bible. Atheists was an expression more suited to their opponents.

The bishop had been quiet to that point. He looked at the crowd. He raised his hand and pointed it at them. 'Away with the atheists!' he proclaimed. His voice was strong and fearless.

'Kill him!' erupted once again from the bloodthirsty onlookers. 'Kill Polycarp!'

The proconsul persisted with his interrogation. 'Swear, and I will release you. Curse Christ,' he said.

Polycarp answered, 'Eighty and six years have I served him, and he has done me no wrong. How then can I blaspheme my King who saved me?'

The proconsul pressed on, saying, 'Take the oath, Polycarp. Say, "Caesar is Lord" and offer a sacrifice of incense. I will let you go.'

'My dear proconsul,' began the bishop. 'If you were to permit me some time, I will gladly instruct you in Christian doctrine. Just appoint the day and listen to what I say.'

'Persuade the people,' said the proconsul grimly. By now, Polycarp struggled to hear his accuser over the loud chants of the people calling for his death.

'I have deemed you worthy of discourse, proconsul,' said Polycarp, 'for we are taught to render to authorities and powers ordained of God's honour as is fitting. But I do not deem this mob worthy that I should defend myself before them.'

'I have wild beasts; if you do not change your mind I will throw you to them,' threatened the proconsul. Ah, he has sunk to the diplomacy of violence, thought Polycarp. He thinks that the power to hurt me will coerce me to betray Christ my King. He is about to be disappointed.

'Give the order for your wild beasts to be brought,' said Polycarp. 'We Christians are not allowed to change our minds from better to worse. But to change from wrong to right is good.'

'If you despise the beasts, unless you change your mind, I shall have you burnt,' warned the proconsul.

'You threaten me with fire that burns for only an hour, and after a little while is extinguished. You are ignorant of the fire of judgement to come, and of everlasting punishment reserved for the ungodly,' responded Polycarp gravely. 'But what are you waiting for? Do what you wish.'

The proconsul realised he was wasting his breath. He conceded that the old man had courage, but the trial was now over. He turned to his herald to announce his finding to the crowd. The herald walked into the middle of the arena. The crowd quietened to hear the proclamation, which would be delivered three times as was the custom.

'Polycarp has confessed himself to be a Christian!' announced the herald. On hearing this news, a deafening roar went up from the crowd. Immediately the people began to clamour for a lion to be let loose on the elderly bishop.

A spokesman for the mob approached Philip the Asiarch, a prominent ruler in the Roman province of Asia and the man in charge of the festival arrangements. He pressed Philip to approve the demand of the people.

'This man is the teacher of Asia, the father of Christians, the destroyer of our gods, and he teaches many of the people not to sacrifice to our gods nor to worship them,' said the spokesman. With such a strong argument, how could the Asiarch refuse the people their wish?

'No lion,' said Philip the Asiarch.

'Why not?' asked the spokesman, clearly disappointed having been refused.

'The Games ended at midday, as they have done so every day of the festival,' reminded the Asiarch. 'It is not lawful for me to release a lion after that time.'

Then the mob shouted, 'Burn him! Burn Polycarp!' Their angry shouts grew louder and louder with each chant. Without waiting for a response from the authorities, some men from the crowd dashed from the stadium and started to collect wood from workshops and bath houses that were close by. Although it was the sabbath, the Jews joined in the work, for they were also bitterly hostile to the spread of Christianity throughout the land.

Hurrying back into the stadium with bundles of wood in their arms, the men began to build a fire. They were egged on by shrieks and howls of approval and satisfaction from the vile mob. By this point, the proconsul and the Asiarch stepped back to allow the brutes their wicked way with Polycarp. The ringleaders seized Polycarp and commanded him to remove his outer clothing. 'Don't worry, bishop, you can warm yourself in the fire we are making for you,' cackled one of the executioners.

The men dragged Polycarp over to the stake. They were about to nail him to it when he cried out, 'Let me be as I am! The Lord God who granted me the strength to endure the fire will grant me also the strength to remain at the pyre unmoved, without being secured with nails.' The men acquiesced and bound his arms with rope, while others piled bundles of wood around his body. Then Polycarp looked to the heavens and started to pray. He thanked God for all his love and mercy to him in his life and for deeming him worthy to be a martyr for the sake of Christ. When he had finished his prayer, the evil men kindled the fire and stepped back to watch the Bishop of Smyrna burn.

The flames blazed up. The lawless mob cheered, then watched in disbelief as the wind blew through the arena causing the fire to move away from Polycarp's body. The flames licked over his head like a perfect wave. Polycarp was not burning. The lynching party became impatient and wanted to end the ordeal quickly. They called a slaughterer, employed to butcher wounded animals in the arena, to stick a knife in the bishop and bring his life to a swift conclusion. The slayer did it without flinching. As the cold blade entered Polycarp's body, he gasped his final breath and died. The onlookers in the stadium roared with delight. At the same time, the church grieved the murder of their treasured pastor and friend.

Polycarp's blood had doused the flames. When his people saw this, they begged for his body, but the authorities would not release it to them, for fear of martyr worship. So, Polycarp's body was burnt by the city's leadership and reduced to ashes. Having done that, the outburst of savagery against the Christian community was over for the time being.

***

The death of Polycarp did not bring about the demise of the church in Smyrna. Roman military strategists believed that the way to defeat an enemy was to target and eliminate the leadership. This would throw the opposing army into chaos by demoralising and disorientating it. Victory would then be assured. Yet, killing Polycarp was never going to destroy the local church in Smyrna. The Lord Jesus made a promise to his apostles. 'I will build my church,' Jesus said, 'and the gates of hell shall not prevail against it.'[1] Many hundreds of years after the death of Polycarp, another wise and godly bishop said this: 'the meaning of this promise is, – that the power of Satan shall never destroy the people of Christ … he shall never bring ruin on the new creation by overthrowing believers. The mystical body of Christ shall never perish nor decay. Though often persecuted, afflicted, distressed and brought low, it shall never come to an end: it shall outlive the wrath of Pharaohs and Roman emperors.'[2]

Jesus said to his followers: 'In me you may have peace. In the world you will have tribulation. But take heart. I have overcome the world.'[3]

---

1. Matthew 16:18.
2. J.C. Ryle, Anglican Bishop of Liverpool from 1880-1900.
3. John 16:33.

***

The Smyrnaean church collected Polycarp's ashes and buried them with honour. A short while after Polycarp's death, some brethren from the church in Phrygia asked for a written account of the martyrdom to be put into a letter and sent to the churches throughout Asia Minor. The secretary of the Smyrnaean church, along with a trusted elder from the church, set about the task of writing it all down. The story of the events of Polycarp's last days was then widely circulated.

Along with other churches throughout the land, the church at Smyrna decided to keep the anniversary of Polycarp's martyrdom. Why? As a joyful festival in remembrance of those who had fought in the contest, and for training and preparation of those who shall do so hereafter.

***

The martyrs were bound, imprisoned, scourged, racked, burnt, rent, butchered — and they multiplied. Augustine, Bishop of Hippo A.D. 354-430, The City of God Book 22.

Appendix One

One man who was trained and prepared for the arduous task of church leadership was Irenaeus. He grieved deeply when he learned of Polycarp's murder at the hands of the Romans. Yet, Irenaeus had a sure and certain hope in the resurrection to eternal life through the Lord Jesus Christ. He knew Polycarp was with the Lord, which is better by far.

Irenaeus remembered those words – 'be faithful unto death' – those words from the Lord Jesus to the church in Smyrna that were engraved into their hearts and embodied by Polycarp. Irenaeus was emboldened by the bishop's noble and faithful witness to Christ till the very end. Indeed, he was now determined to become one of those who would fight the good fight. For a while now, he had wondered if he should serve the Lord as a missionary in France.

All his friends at church agreed that Polycarp was blessed with a long life of quiet, constructive work for the Master. The old bishop's life was an inspiration to many of them, who knew him as a pastor of God's flock in Smyrna and as a friend. Irenaeus believed that his death was an example to the church of how to die well.

As he grew older, Irenaeus often reminisced of his days in the Smyrnaean church. He remembered fondly and often wondered what Polycarp would say to some of the people and heresies that Irenaeus was contending against. About half a century after Polycarp's death, Irenaeus had a problem with an old friend who, alongside him, sat at Polycarp's feet and learned the gospel of salvation from him as a young man. His name was Florinus. Irenaeus wished the old Bishop of Smyrna was there to advise him. Still, he had a good idea what Polycarp would say and do.

Irenaeus decided to write a letter to Florinus because his friend had lapsed into false teaching about the gospel. He recalled the days when they had both listened to Polycarp as an older and mature Christian man:

> I clearly remember the events of that time, Irenaeus
> wrote, so that I can even tell the place where the
> blessed Polycarp used to sit and discourse, and his
> goings out and in, and the manner of his life, and the
> appearance of his body, and the discourse which he
> used to describe his conversation with John and with
> others who had seen the Lord; and as he remembered
> their words, and what were the things he had heard
> from them about the Lord and about his miracles
> and about his teaching – as having received from
> the eyewitnesses the facts concerning the life of the

Word, Jesus – Polycarp used to describe all these things even then, through the mercy of God given to me, did I eagerly listen, remembering them not on paper, but in my heart. And by the grace of God I always genuinely reflect on them: and I can testify before that, if that Polycarp had heard any of the things that you are now saying, he would have shouted out, and stopped his ears, and said as was his custom, 'Dear Lord, to what times have you kept me that I should endure this nonsense!' Then he would have fled from the place where sitting or standing he had heard such words.

These remembrances often cheered Irenaeus's heart when it was heavy with trials and sufferings. He hoped it would help his friend come to his senses and proclaim the true gospel of Jesus from the Bible. Polycarp's influence in his own life impressed upon him the seriousness of handling the Word of God well. He was grateful to the old bishop for that. It was an invaluable lesson for his own ministry in France, where he did end up serving the Lord. When he was appointed the Bishop of Lyon, Irenaeus thought Polycarp would be pleased were he to be alive.

Irenaeus thanked the Lord often for his mercy in the past, and for the provision of such godly men as Polycarp who helped mentor and shape him into the man he had become. Irenaeus was martyred for his faith in Jesus Christ in A.D. 200 during the reign of the Roman Emperor Septimus Severus.

Appendix Two

Throughout this book Polycarp has conversations on issues that he felt strongly about, for example, the Scriptures being the Word of God, persecution of the Church, and his dislike of false teachers and heresy. I have paraphrased some of Polycarp's views for the purpose of good conversation, but they can be found in Polycarp's 'Letter to the Philippians'and the 'Letter of the Smyrnaeans', which are found in the books, *A New Eusebius – Documents illustrating the history of the Church to A.D. 337* revised by W.H.C. Frend, (SPCK, New Revision, 1987) and *The Apostolic Fathers* by J.B. Lightfoot (Baker Book House, edited and completed into one volume by J.R. Harmer, 1987). *Pionius – The Life of Polycarp* from J.B. Lightfoot's *The Apostolic Fathers, Vol. III* (www.tertullian.org), was also a helpful section concerning Polycarp's views and background.

In writing this story, other history books were a great help, such as *The Spreading Flame – The Paternoster*

Church History Vol. 1' by F.F. Bruce (Paternoster 1958); 'Life in the Early Church A.D. 33 to 313' by A.E. Weslford (S.P.C.K., 1955); *The History of Christianity* (Lion, 1990); *The Early Church* by Henry Chadwick (Penguin Books, 1993); *The Story of the Church* by A.M. Renwick and A.M. Harman (InterVarsity Press, 1996); *The Early Church – From the beginnings to 461* by W.H.C Frend (SCM Press Ltd, 1991); and *The Encyclopaedia Britannica* (London 1994).

To help me understand more about the ancient world of Polycarp, I found the following books useful: *Looking at Ancient History* by R.J. Unstead (Morrison and Gibb, 1960); *Ancient World* by Rupert Matthews (Miles Kelly, 2007); *Daily Life in Ancient Rome* by Jerome Carcopino (Hale University Press, 1977); and *Everyday Life in New Testament Times* by A.C. Bouquet (Batsford, 1954).

The website www.newadvent.org was useful too, because it has lots of articles about church history, including articles about Ignatius and Irenaeus who feature in this story. The books, *A New Eusebius* and *The Apostolic Fathers* mentioned above also include writings of these men.

Polycarp:
Timeline

A.D.

34-35   Conversion of Paul the apostle (Acts 9).

47 or 48:   Famine in Jerusalem.

49   Council of Jerusalem (Acts 15).

57   Paul's letter to the Romans.

65   Paul executed in Rome under Emperor Nero's persecution of Christians.

70   Birth of Polycarp.

80-84   John the apostle writes his Gospel in the early 80s.

90-94   John the apostle writes his Epistles in the early 90s.

96   Revelation of John on the island of Patmos during the reign of Emperor Domitian (81-96).

100   John the apostle dies in Ephesus.

110   Death of Ignatius in Rome.

120   Papias becomes Bishop of Hierapolis in southwestern Turkey.

130   Birth of Irenaeus.

140   Marcion travels to Rome to try to convince the Church of his views. He argued that ten letters of Paul and one Gospel, a mutilated

version of Luke, comprised the proper NT canon. He was excommunicated as a heretic.

155   Polycarp visits Anicetus in Rome to discuss the Paschal Controversy.

156   Death of Polycarp in Smyrna.

202   Irenaeus, Bishop of Lyon, dies during the persecution of Christians under Emperor Lucius Septimus Severus.

Thinking Further Topics

Chapter 1: The Hideout

Polycarp wanted his enemies to know the saving grace of Jesus Christ. He prayed for his enemies all the time. Was Polycarp right to do this? Do you pray for your enemies? What do you pray; that they may know Jesus personally, or that Jesus would destroy them?
Read Matthew 5:44-45 and Romans 12:9-21.

Chapter 2: A Letter to Smyrna

Polycarp reminisced about the apostle John and the empty tomb of Jesus. Is Jesus alive or was his body stolen by someone? Why is the answer to this question important to Christians?
Read Matthew 28:11-15, 1 Corinthians 15:13-19, John 20:19-23, and 1 John 1:1-3.

Chapter 3: Kallisto

Polycarp felt it was his duty as a Christian to look after widows, orphans, and the poor. Do you feel this way too? If so, why? What can you do to help the poor?
Read Matthew 5:42 and 25:31-40.

Chapter 4: Fierce Wolves

As the Bishop of Smyrna, Polycarp's duty was to look after God's people. Sometimes he had to fight against false teachers who taught something different to the

gospel of Jesus. Do you think it is important to contend for the truth of the Bible? If not, why not?
Read Titus 1:9.

Chapter 5: Martyrdom

When Polycarp met Ignatius in Smyrna, Ignatius was on his way to Rome to be executed for his faith in Jesus Christ. Do you think it was right for Ignatius to stand firm in what he believed, or should he have been a bit more flexible, given the fact that his life was in danger?
Read 1 Corinthians 16:13, Galatians 5:1, Philippians 1:27 and 2 Thessalonians 2:13-17.

Chapter 6: A Visit to Rome

In his conversation with the young Irenaeus, Polycarp spoke of the cost of being a follower of the Lord Jesus Christ. Are you ready to bear the cost of following Jesus, even if it means that you will be going against the flow of the world?
Read 2 Timothy 4:8, James 1:12 and 1 Peter 5:4.

Chapter 7: Good Friends

Polycarp spoke about the Christian's fight against Satan. The Bible refers to Satan as a liar, a tempter, and an accuser. He tempts people into sin by lying to them. When we fall for his lies he stands before God and accuses us. The gospel robs him of this power. What does God give us to make us ready for the battle? What must we do at all times?
Read Ephesians 6:10-18 to help you think about these things.

Chapter 8: The Escape Plan

When the soldiers finally found Polycarp, he asked them for time to pray. Why is prayer so important for Christians? When and how often do you pray to God? If you do not pray, why not? Remember, 'prayer is the chief exercise of faith' (John Calvin, Church Reformer). Read Matthew 6:5-13, Colossians 4:2 and 1 Thessalonians 5:16-18.

Chapter 9: Faithful unto Death

The authorities tried to coerce Polycarp to sacrifice to Caesar and declare that 'Caesar is Lord'. Polycarp refused to do this, knowing that he would be executed if he did not. What do you think about other religions in the world? Are they all equally valid? Why do Christians say it is vitally important to worship only Christ?

Read Exodus 20:3, John 14:6, and 1 John 5:20 to start you thinking about these things.

TRAIL BLAZERS

• Patrick of Ireland •
THE BOY WHO FORGAVE

K. C. Murdarasi

Patrick of Ireland

The Boy who Forgave
by K.C. Murdarasi

Saint, Slave or Scholar? Patrick of Ireland is known as all three but who is he really? Let K.C. Murdarasi bring to light the real life of this father of the Christian faith. Kidnapped from his home and family as a young boy you would think forgiveness would have been far from his mind.

Yet with God's grace Patrick returned to the land of his captivity where he preached the Good News of Jesus Christ to slaves and kings alike and left a legacy of faith that would last for centuries.

ISBN: 978-1-78191-677-3

Although she is best known for her time on the mission field in Ecuador, Elisabeth Elliot went on to become a vibrant role model for valiant, godly women all over the world. Follow her journey from the jungles of the Amazon, where she faced the tragic death of her first husband, to the lecture halls and radio shows of the culture wars, where she stood as a strong defender of God's Word.

ISBN: 978-1-5271-0161-6

OTHER BOOKS IN THE
TRAIL BLAZERS SERIES

Augustine, The Truth Seeker
ISBN 978-1-78191-296-6
John Calvin, After Darkness Light
ISBN 978-1-78191-550-9
Fanny Crosby, The Blind Girl's Song
ISBN 978-1-78191-163-1
John Knox, The Sharpened Sword
ISBN 978-1-78191-057-3
Eric Liddell, Finish the Race
ISBN 978-1-84550-590-5
Martin Luther, Reformation Fire
ISBN 978-1-78191-521-9
Robert Moffat, Africa's Brave Heart
ISBN 978-1-84550-715-2
D.L. Moody, One Devoted Man
ISBN 978-1-78191-676-6
Mary of Orange, At the Mercy of Kings
ISBN 978-1-84550-818-0
Patrick of Ireland: The Boy who Forgave
ISBN: 978-1-78191-677-3
John Stott, The Humble Leader
ISBN 978-1-84550-787-9
Ulrich Zwingli, Shepherd Warrior
ISBN 978-1-78191-803-6

For a full list of Trail Blazers, please see our
website: www.christianfocus.com
All Trail Blazers are available as e-books